The Warde

A Lifetime in N

Tim Russell

Quantock Hills 1997

1

Preface

When I first started compiling memories and anecdotes for this book, I had intended to write solely about my twenty-five years spent as the Warden on the Quantock Hills. However, it gradually became apparent that the tragic and untimely loss of my dad in 1975 – when I was fourteen years old and just getting to know him properly – had an extremely traumatic effect on me.

Sadly, counselling was uncommon in the mid-seventies: you just 'got on with it'. I recognise now that rarely talking about my father and locking away this pain for so long has, at times, held me back emotionally in my adult life. Recalling both my rural childhood and my career through the process of writing has been wonderfully cathartic and a valuable, unexpected, healing process. I am now able to celebrate properly my father's memory and his importance to me.

I dedicate this book to my late father Colin Russell (1934–1975), who introduced me to the joy of nature and the beauty of the natural world. To my mother Pam for allowing my brothers and I to roam free and have adventures; to my two daughters, Rosie and Ellie, who persisted in persuading me to put my memories into written words; to my partner Tor for her patience and beautiful artwork; and to my stepson Ben for allowing me to stay young at heart and getting me back on my old skateboard!

I would like to thank nature writers Sir John Lister-Kaye OBE, Stephen Moss and Miriam Darlington for their helpful advice and encouragement during the early stages in putting this book together, Martin Hesp (West Country writer and journalist) for his useful comments, and Lily Hill and Sue Viccars (freelance editor and writer) for their assistance with proof reading and editing.

Disclaimer
This book is a recollection of my childhood and career – but I have to consider other people's privacy, so a few names have been changed to protect their identities.

First published 2022 – Barn Owl Press
ISBN 978-1-3999-3484-8

Tim Russell - timrussell61@hotmail.com

Cover & illustrations - Tor Allen www.torallenillustrator.com
Book cover – Murmuration at Slapton Ley.

Many thanks to the printers, mixam.co.uk, for their excellent customer service.

Chapters:

Prelude

After three or four attempts I managed to jump up and grab onto the stumpy dead branches partway up the trunk of the larch tree. I pulled myself up and began to climb. I had often looked up to the wood from our garden and seen this tree's pointed crown swaying proudly above the more rounded oaks and sycamores below.

I was definitely a tree climber. I'd had a few falls, but I'd conquered some giants in a fairly naive and fearless way. This time I was convinced that I could climb to the very top of the tree, out above the canopy of the wood. It was surprisingly easy to climb, a living ladder, and I gained height quickly. I made sure that I held and stood on the branches as close to the trunk as possible just as my father (a rock climber) had taught me, with never fewer than 'three points of contact'.

As I climbed, I gazed through the cool, dappled layers of the wood. I saw the aerial-runway he had made for us to fly through the trees, like shrieking goshawks, and the tree house he had built for us in the old, silver-barked, spreading rowan. It felt good to be by myself, in my own space, time to just be me, alone with my own thoughts, comforted by the living green blanket.

The trees were coming into full leaf. It was half a year now since my father's tragic death in a road collision. I was a confused, traumatised individual, not quite fifteen.

Am I still a child? Am I supposed to be grown up and sensible now? How could I show support to my mother and two younger brothers yet still keep my emerging teenage independence? Was I allowed to cry, to show emotion and not be embarrassed?

How could I stay strong? How could I just be me? 'You're Man of the Household now' Uncle John had said to me as he patted me on the back – but I didn't want to be, didn't know how to be – how was I expected to be? My life wasn't meant to be like this. It felt unfair and unmanageable.

I carried on climbing. The tree was much thinner near the top and started swaying under my weight. I was scared, I was shaking, I could barely move; I knew a fall now would most likely kill me. One more nerve-racking pull brought me out above the leafy canopy and into the light, the bright warm sunshine and gentle breeze. I held on for dear life: a whole green world lay below me and stretched to hazy, distant horizons. It was breath-taking – one of those moments you never forget.

I took in the views, many miles south across the wide Shropshire plain to the humpbacked Wrekin and the misty-blue Shropshire Hills. Turning my head carefully, not wanting to lose balance or concentration, I could pick out the rugged Breiddens and the rolling border country. Behind me, to the west, the Berwyns and the more distant hills of mid Wales.

This was the country my parents had moved to from the Midlands. This was the landscape that we were introduced to as children and taught to love and appreciate.

I was dearly going to miss my father, his great knowledge, his solidity, his protective presence, guidance and humour. What were our lives going to be like now? What a waste to have died so young, to have achieved so much, to have had such an influence and to have so much more to give in the fields of environmental education and conservation – and, fundamentally, just being a dad.

How was I going to ensure his legacy remained? Would I be able to pick up and carry his baton, his inherent love for the natural world?

Chapter One: Conservation is in the blood

My speeding Land Rover bounced across the yellow, sunburnt field towards the flaming hillside. If I could locate a suitable spot for the fire brigade to access this remote corner of the hills, we might just stop the wildfire spreading into the deep gorse and scrub on Great Bear and losing it up the valley. As I raced across the hardened earth towards the furthest corner of the field the vehicle came to a sudden, sickening stop, then slowly began to lean over to one side. The blue sky was now framed weirdly at forty-five degrees through the dusty windscreen, and I came to the terrible realisation – I was sinking!

With my concentration focused on the hill fire I had inadvertently driven onto a slurry pit, its once tell-tale, bright green skin now the same burnt yellow as the rest of the field. The Land Rover was slumped like a wounded beast; I began to panic. I couldn't open the driver's door, the vehicle's angle was now ninety degrees more than it should have been, and it was getting darker inside my metal casket. I squirmed out of the driver's seat and headed towards the blue square of sky filling the passenger window. With great relief I managed to open it and clamber out. I stood on the door rather shakily, then jumped clear onto firmer ground. For a few moments I gazed at the vehicle in shock and disbelief – only a fraction of the near side still visible. Did that really just happen? Someday, I thought, I should write down and share these countryside wardening adventures.

Before diving into the details of my life as a warden – particularly the twenty-five years spent on the Quantock Hills in Somerset – I should probably explain how I got to that stage of my life. Much of my interest in nature came from my father. He had been a warden too, but of a different kind, although his fundamental message was the same: learn as much as you can from nature, love the countryside, help to protect it and enthuse others to do the same.

In my early years he was head of biology at Ellesmere College in Shropshire. We lived in a tied property, St Mary's Cottage, on St John's Hill; I have fond memories of walking to school down this narrow street chanting the hits of the day – such as 'Yellow Submarine' and 'Lily the Pink' – with my schoolmates. My father would occasionally take me to school on his beloved pushbike; I had a footrest, and a small red plastic saddle attached to the crossbar.

Ellesmere is located in what is known as Shropshire's Lake District (on account of its glacial meres). It's a lovely red-brick town with stunning Georgian properties, some looking like giant doll's houses. The old Shropshire Union canal network has an important junction and wharf here, now popular with canal boats used for holidays or simply alternative places to live. As I write this my mother still lives in Ellesmere, in its oldest surviving cottage, a half-timbered property near the church overlooking The Mere. When I visit now, I often stroll down to the mere and into the wonderful lakeside park of Cremorne Gardens. I pass the contorted yew tree that I used to climb in as a youngster (as generations of children have done before and since, including my own) and try to envisage my five-year-old self excitedly clambering amongst those shiny, well-worn lower branches, more than half a century ago. Something else I remember from that time is the 1967 foot-and-mouth epidemic and seeing huge pyres of burning cattle as we drove towards Oswestry in our dark green Triumph Herald estate.

My father became the Warden at Preston Montford Field Studies Centre near Shrewsbury in 1973. His main role was to manage the centre for the Field Studies Council and to teach students on residential courses how to study nature in the field and the importance of environmental education and conservation. It is from him that I learnt to love wildlife and the richness of the Shropshire landscape. Growing up as a field-centre child and being free to roam and explore the countryside and to absorb, almost unknowingly, the 'environmental understanding for all' ethos of the organisation, was a rare privilege.

Our family lived in the warden's flat, a first-floor apartment in the old Georgian house of Preston Montford Hall, set in forty acres of its own parkland down a long cattle-gridded drive. It all seemed rather grand. My younger brother Mike and I particularly loved exploring the steeply wooded banks of the River Severn which edged the property and would spend hours outdoors before returning home for tea. If we were back in time, we were allowed to ring the bell which hung in a tower at the top of the hall, pulling on its long thin rope to summon residential students or course participants to supper.

Exploring the house was fun, too, particularly over the Christmas period when we had the run of it to ourselves: the cool, damp, spooky cellar, the labyrinth of corridors and landings and the grand, dark oak timber staircase to slide down in pillowcases. One small room was used solely for storing mattresses and this became our 'bouncy room', sneakily accessed through a small door from the playroom in our flat. On the outside of the building there was a metal fire escape, probably added in the 1960s. We used to climb to the very top and throw off our Action Men, adorned with home-made parachutes that never seemed to work, so they usually landed horribly contorted on the gravel below.

Paul and Annie's top floor flat had access to the fire escape. Paul was the field centre's freshwater ecologist, and if he saw us, he would beckon us in to show us his amazing collection of tropical fish in exotically lit, colourful aquariums. Annie, his wife and centre cook, would occasionally treat us to chocolate-covered Club biscuits or Bandit bars from the main pantry – happy days!

Every now and then we would use the fire escape to gain access to the sloped and channelled 'roof world' of the hall, exploring this hidden and forbidden place of mossy, leaded valleys, lichen-covered slates and tiled crests. One of my favourite places to dare myself to go to and sit was next to the wooden bell tower. I don't think anyone ever knew... especially my parents.

We had a rather demented Welsh Pony called Dinky, who was a nightmare! We could only catch him by gradually cornering him with a long rope. He used to try to dismount us by scraping us against telegraph poles or barbed wire fences, and would stop short at a full canter or turn at ninety degrees, throwing us off onto the hard ground. He was also prone to suddenly bolting at full pace with one (or sometimes more) of us on his back, and seemed to enjoy purposefully standing on our feet when we attempted to groom him. My pride and joy was a second-hand green Raleigh Chopper bike (I wish I still had it – it would probably be quite sought after now). I used to cycle everywhere on it until it was stolen from near my school bus stop. At thirteen I learnt to drive my father's old blue Land Rover station wagon across the fields, having to slide off the seat a little to depress the clutch.

Being a young teenager in the early 1970s was fun; we were 'free-range' and hardly ever indoors unless it was raining or *The Banana Splits*, *Planet of The Apes* or of course *Blue Peter* was on the telly. Sometimes TV theme tunes from long ago swim back into my memory and remind me of the other programmes from my childhood: *Robinson Crusoe, Champion the Wonder Horse, Thunderbirds, Captain Scarlett, Top Cat, The Double Deckers, Hong Kong Phooey, Star Trek* and, later, *MASH*. The change from black and white to colour was exciting and memorable, although I don't think we had our first colour TV until the late seventies!

Dad would occasionally bring orphaned wild animals home for us to nurse back to health. We had a kestrel we called Falco, a couple of hare leverets, a fox cub called Tag… and I can remember feeding young bats milk from a small pipette. I was devastated when the fox disappeared and spent days looking for him on my bike. One of my very earliest memories is sharing the back seat of my father's Morris Minor convertible with a goat! I have some old photographs of me, aged about two, with a squirrel and a badger called Tommy Brock. Menageries seemed to be the norm, and I can easily relate to the childhood described in Gerald Durrell's book *My Family and Other Animals*.

Not long after we had moved back to Sweeney Mountain from Preston Montford my father was tragically killed in a traffic collision in November 1975 on his way back home from delivering an evening lecture in Shrewsbury. He had just agreed to write a New Naturalist Series book on *The Otter*, a threatened species for which he had helped gain protection.

In his eulogy to my father, Charles Sinker (the previous field centre Warden) wrote:

He was a very talented teacher, equally at home in the classroom or lecture hall, in the laboratory or in the field. With that rare sensibility towards an audience which enabled him to adapt treatment and style to any age group, he could transmit knowledge and the joy of inquiry to infants as well as sixth form pupils, to teachers in training, adult amateurs and students of the Open University alike. Rigorous as he was in his appraisal of scientific methods, yet he carried his scholarship lightly; he served his serious and weighty subject with the salt and spice of humour. Colin Russell was a good biologist in the formal sense, but it is as an outstanding field naturalist and an ardent advocate of nature conservation that he will be best remembered. His knowledge of nature was wide, and he was never happier than when leading an enthusiastic class in the field, especially around the Meres or in the hill country of Shropshire and North Wales. He chose to specialise in mammals and was an acknowledged expert on the otter and an authority on bats and badgers. Energy, conviction, eloquence and charm were among his outstanding attributes...

I was, and still am, very proud of his work with the Field Studies Council, Shropshire Wildlife Trust, Mammal Society, World Wildlife Fund and the Gavin Maxwell Otter fund, working alongside friends and colleagues including Peter Scott, Phil Drabble, Richard Fitter, Lord Cranbrook, Ernest Neal (The Badger Man), Ian Mercer (Slapton warden and Dartmoor's first officer), Charles Sinker (botanist), Henry Disney (entomologist) and other conservationists during the agriculturally intensive and destructive times of the 1970s.

During the fifties and throughout the sixties these people were true naturalists and conservation pioneers, helping to plant the seeds of nature conservation and environmental education at a time when our National Parks were only just coming into being. I remember Dad showing me recently grubbed-out hedgerows and being driven down the M5 on our way to visit Ernest Neal in Somerset, saddened and shocked at seeing the skeletal rows of dead and dying elm trees as we travelled south. Half a century later it is just as disheartening to see skeletons of trees suffering from ash die-back in our countryside. The elm and the ash, two of Britain's finest native trees, with centuries of use and folklore, being lost from our landscape and, quite possibly, our collective memory.

My father was born in 1934, was five by the start of the Second World War and just ten when it was over. Being a young boy in Coventry must have been harrowing during its blitz and I can imagine his great relief when the war was over, and he could get out and explore the leafy Warwickshire countryside on his bike. Like many young boys of his generation, collecting birds' eggs was an almost obsessive hobby and I have wonderful excerpts from his meticulous nature diaries extolling a sensitive and respectful approach to this pastime (and recounting regular run-ins with gruff gamekeepers).

From the 1950s to the mid-sixties he kept detailed observational diaries of badger behaviour in the woods (such as Stoneymoor Wood) near Kenilworth.

Sadly, the wonderful old woodlands that he explored (for example Cubbington Woods), island remnants of Shakespeare's ancient Forest of Arden, are being ripped apart for HS2, one of the government's latest vanity projects: a high-speed rail link which will cost UK taxpayers around £100 billion and threatens hundreds of areas of beautiful and diverse wildlife just to shave 20 minutes off the journey from Birmingham to London. Avenues of ancient oaks along the Roman Fosse Way have been felled and Balsall Common, very dear to my dad, flattened, our countryside heritage under threat as never before.

He studied zoology and botany at Bangor University in North Wales, the first of his family to go to university. He was a keen rock climber and loved the mountains. He'd take us hill walking in the Lake District and Snowdonia where it always seemed to be raining, and I fondly remember being chivvied along in our sodden Peter Storm kagools by promises of Kendal Mint Cake when we reached 'the next ridge'.

During our time living at the field centre, we were joined for a while by two of our cousins, Mark and Mike Harold, who had recently lost their father Martyn to cancer.

I can remember Uncle Martyn taking my father and I for a spin in his brand-new Jensen Interceptor. I loved its exciting name, sleek shape and beautiful design. Compared to our Hillman Minx its multi-dialled dashboard resembled the cockpit of a plane, but it felt more like a spaceship to me. It was the first time I'd been 100 miles an hour in a car – I'll never forget it.

Mark and Mike soon came to love the freedom of the field centre's country estate and I can recall one particular adventure we shared when the River Severn broke its banks. We tied ourselves together with a long rope (Mark's idea) and waded waist-deep through the flooded woods, swept along by the force of the swollen river and holding onto each other and tree trunks, like a swamp scene from the movie *Southern Comfort*. We were caught later while trying to wring our soaked and muddy clothing out with an old mangle. Boy were we in trouble – how dangerous was that? I recently learnt that it was due to my father's influence that my cousins both pursued long and influential careers in conservation, for the National Trust and Greenpeace respectively.

My younger brother Mike has also contributed to nature conservation through his award-winning landscape designs and creating wonderful wildlife gardens from his base in the Shropshire Hills. My youngest brother, Simon, who's also very keen on the outdoors (often on his mountain bike), lives amongst the pine-clothed, sandstone hills near Nesscliffe, enjoying stunning sunset views to the Breidden Hills and the bumpy Welsh border from the top of The Cliffe.

By the time I was in my late teens I knew that I wanted to work to help protect the environment; it was in my blood, after all, and somehow inside I felt that it was my duty to carry on my father's work. It was my best friend Dewi Morris who inadvertently cemented this career-path realisation when he bought me an old green enamel pin-badge from a junk shop as a sixteenth birthday present. Its gold letters proudly stated: 'Snowdonia National Park Warden'... 'Now, there's a job!' I thought. I still have that old badge (probably one of the first made for the Park in the 1950s) and it is one of my treasured possessions along with some worked flints, a polar bear skull and a collection of old bottles.

Dewi introduced me to collecting old bottles. I'd misheard him initially and thought he said, 'Let's go buckle digging', so it didn't sound too much fun. Anyway, it soon became apparent that we were looking for old bottles and we began digging up old tips and rummaging around abandoned farmsteads. We got quite hooked on this newfound hobby – a great excuse to explore and trespass – and over the years we managed to accrue individual collections of some wonderful Victorian bottles along with some old enamel advertising signs and other paraphernalia. We would venture out into the countryside on our pushbikes with spade and rucksack and come home filthy, tired and with rucksacks bulging with old glass and pottery. It may seem a rather strange hobby to be almost addicted to as a young teenager, but the thrill of gently pulling a complete Victorian bottle from the sides of a hole in the ground was surprisingly satisfying.

A good 90% or so of the bottles were broken, so a complete specimen was a great find, especially an old Codd bottle with its glass marble intact. Victorian and Edwardian children would purposefully smash these bottles for the marble inside to play 'Alley', so they were rare and treasured finds.

I still have the very first old bottle I ever dug up with Dewi when I was about thirteen, a small, irregular, aqua-coloured bottle with a twisted neck and bubbles and tears in the glass, now on display in a kitchen cabinet along with a few others collected over the years. Perhaps the compulsion to collect and arrange is a symptom of PTSD; sub-consciously dealing with trauma by transforming it into some semblance of order.

For the first few years after we lost Dad, my mother would take us to stay with the Wilsons, long-term friends who lived in the old Bishop's Palace on the Menai Straits in Anglesey. They had all grown up in the West Midlands and Dad and Ian were both biology graduates from Bangor. They rode to North Wales up the old A5 on their motorbikes in the mid-fifties and soon fell in love with the dramatic mountain and coastal scenery. Ian stayed there (becoming a professor at the university) and was able to purchase the Bishop's Palace with its stunning views to Snowdonia across the rushing, tidal waters.

The property lies halfway between the two bridges on the north side of the straits, a little to the west of Church Island. The bottom of Ian's land (known by his family as The End) was hugely enticing to us teenagers and we soon discovered that, at low tide, the thick black, oozy mud held treasure! The Victorian residents of the 'palace' must have been wealthy as we found wonderful toothpaste lids and hand-thrown earthenware ink jars in the muddy craters of the Somme-like landscape that the retreating tide revealed. It is difficult to describe the excitement of gently freeing one of these decorative lids from the black, stinking mud as clear and clean as the day it was thrown away, well over a hundred years ago.

How many racing tides had passed over its sodden, sunless spot? How none of us ever got tetanus or were trapped in the mud I will never know. I still have some of those old toothpaste lids; they bring back happy memories of those mud-larking expeditions on the Menai Straits.

Despite the trauma of recently losing our father we made the best of what we had, and I have particularly fond memories of those Anglesey days: the comfort and relaxing space of the huge house and its mesmerising views to the snow-capped mountains across the white, rushing water and distant pines, the low-tide explorations and the ever-present, piping call of the oystercatchers. When my own daughters were children, I introduced them to the place. We skateboarded down the smooth tarmac road to Church Island and (along with their cousins) buried a time capsule containing their poems and sketches down at The End in 2000. I guess it is still there by the little stone bench that looks out across the water just above the old, orange-lichen covered sea wall.

After Dad died, Dewi's father Dilwyn (ex-head teacher and mountain leader) very kindly took us boys under his wing and introduced us to the wonders of the nearby Welsh mountains through wild camping and exploring.

I had come to love these rugged places: the Rhinogs, with their rocky lunar landscape and wild goats and the Aran Range with their magnificent views. Aran Fawddwy is still my favourite mountain, the highest British mountain south of Yr Wyddfa (Snowdon). The view from the summit is extensive, covering most of the mountain ranges of North Wales and as far south as the Brecon Beacons and Pembrokeshire peninsula. On a clear day you can make out the Lake District fells in England and the Wicklow Mountains in Ireland.

Most visits, however, were to the closer and more subtle hills of the Berwyns and the area around Dilwyn's childhood home of Llangynog, where we also explored the long-abandoned slate caverns. Dilwyn always had wonderful tales to tell of the local history, translating the barely pronounceable place names into their English equivalents: 'cave of the red-haired bandits', 'place of eagles', 'wolf rock' or 'valley of the bear'... our imagination was filled with this wild Wales of times long ago. Along with George Burrow's 1854 book *Wild Wales: Its People, Language and Scenery* he always carried a packet of mint imperials and would 'economically' hand them out when we were flagging. It all seemed rather Tolkienesque: the landscapes, the folklore and even Dilwyn himself who, with his white hair, is still affectionately known as Gandalf.

Although I have spent most of my adult life in the southwest, my heart still belongs to the rolling hills of The Marches border country where my formative years were spent and where my love of nature and the landscape was truly forged: a Shropshire Lad from those 'Blue Remembered Hills'. After the long drive from Devon, I still get excited as I anticipate the wonderful views where the M54 ends through a broad stone cutting, the road swings north towards Shrewsbury and the landscape of my childhood comes into view, the Shropshire hills and the distant Welsh border… it really takes me back.

Chapter Two: Sweeney Mountain

Much of my early childhood was spent roaming the area around where we then lived – on Sweeney Mountain – close to the old market town of Oswestry. This is a hilltop with far-reaching vistas, overlooking the Shropshire plain and the bumpy hills of the border country. Close by were the wooded slopes of Llanymynech Hill and the valley that leads into Wales via the village of Porthywaen ('gateway to the hills').

Sweeney Mountain was made up of small, steep-sided limestone meadows and woodlands, drystone walls and long-forgotten, overgrown quarries that nature had reclaimed. It was a wonderful place to explore and my brothers, cousins and I spent as much time as we could outdoors in this intimate landscape. We would occasionally dam the nearby ford, raising its depth and width dramatically – to the annoyance of any motorist attempting to cross it!

Every now and then I would climb to the very top of the mature larch tree that popped its head above the canopy of the other trees in the little wood that separated our house from my cousins'. The base of the tree grew in a gentle curve, allowing access to its ladder-like branches; but at the top it was frighteningly thin, and I would hang on for dear life as the tree swayed with my weight in the breeze. No one could see me; I was King of the Canopy, and I could survey the expanse of my childhood realm to every point of the compass. The views of the surrounding countryside were breath-taking, as was the precarious height of the tree. If only my mother knew…

On the very summit of Sweeney Mountain, with commanding 360-degree views, was the 'haunted house': dark, abandoned and Marie Celeste-like with antlered trophies and faded pictures still adorning some of the walls. This must have been the old hunting lodge to the Sweeney Estate; it was Gothic in appearance, giving it a spooky silhouette, and had underground vaults, probably the old game larders. In our early days we would dare ourselves to visit this hilltop folly, sneaking through the tangled woods and pushing open the creaky old doors into the dank darkness, trying to avoid noisily cracking the broken glass on the dusty floor, alerting any resident ghosts to our trespass. We loved to introduce unsuspecting friends to its seductive, sinister charms – our very own Scooby Doo adventures!

Wild Wood lay to the southwest of our house, and from a distance it always looked extensive, unexplored and enticing. In its depths were abandoned quarrymen's cottages with collapsing outbuildings and overgrown, nettled gardens which we would regularly explore, unearthing old bottles, rusty gin-traps, old metal-studded quarrymen's boots and other abandoned relics. A herd of pigs rough-grazed here. We used to throw stones at them to attract their attention and then climb the trees to avoid their angered charges. I used to wonder whether the name Sweeney was derived from 'swiney', a place where pigs foraged in the woods.

Not long after we moved there the first of the woodlands abutting our property was clear-felled, then every couple of years or so another was felled, and then another. The countryside, our world and playground, was quickly changing. It all seemed very wrong, unfair – and completely out of our control.

Near the track to our house, round a couple of bends in the steeply banked lane, lived 'Fred the Crossing'. He was an old farmer who lived alone and always wore a long beige parlour coat and very well-worn, turned-over Wellington boots. When it was raining, he draped an old hessian sack over his head and shoulders. To us small boys he was quite frightening; he had a weather-beaten face criss-crossed with a thousand red blood vessels and protruding, bloodshot eyes, rather similar in appearance to Uncle Fester from the Addams Family!

He lived on a smallholding that straddled the old horse-drawn railway that once carried stone from the quarries. He had a few cows, a pig for fattening in the sty, free-range chickens and a few geese patrolling the yard.

My brother Mike and I would be sent down to his farm occasionally for fresh milk and eggs. We quite enjoyed the walk and dawdled for most of it. I can still remember the steep hedgebanks along the lane, covered in primroses and cowslips. We would collect the thick, creamy milk in a big jug and carry the cluster of eggs back in our coat pockets. In our first conversation with him he asked us where we had just moved from: 'Ellesmere,' we chirped. 'Ahh, they'm all blummin' cuckoos over there,' he said. Ellesmere was more than ten miles away, so another world as far as Fred was concerned. I remember one occasion when my brother looked down at an egg in his hand and pulled a face: it was covered in hen poo and had a tiny feather still stuck to it. 'Hey mon, you gotta eat a bit o' dirt afore e die,' said Fred. Not a bad philosophy for life, I suppose.

It was along these flower-fringed lanes that we would occasionally take our goat, Heidi, for walks, allowing her to graze the sweet vegetation in the verges and hedgerows as we went. It all seemed so normal; two youngsters just ambling along with a floppy-eared goat in tow. How wonderfully rural, carefree, idyllic and naive it all was. The year 1970 could have passed for 1870, or even 1770 for that matter: timeless, no routine, no agenda.

Those innocent days seemed to last forever. No responsibilities or future to plan, no clock to watch, embracing each new youthful day as it came along.

I can easily identify with Laurie Lee's rural childhood idyll in sleepy Slad, beautifully described in *Cider with Rosie*.

Like him, I can recall my own early school days pretty well. The majority of these were spent at The National School in Welsh Walls, Oswestry. Unlike the modern, light and airy primary school I attended in Ellesmere this was a rather sombre, grey stone Victorian building with separate entrances and playgrounds for boys and girls and high windows so no children could be distracted by the lure of the great outdoors.

I have very fond memories of this traditional school; we played 'British Bulldog' (while the girls did skipping), would link arms and pace around the playground calling out 'All in for Army', gathering more and more recruits until the bell went for the end of playtime. We dared each other to venture into the dark and damp of the World War Two air-raid shelter and traversed the rough stone walls of the school 'escaping our Colditz', doing our best to avoid the patrolling, uniformed, Gestapo-like dinner ladies on playground duty who would make us stand muted in the hall as punishment for our wall-climbing escapades until lunch break was over. I was sent to 'Bonzo' (Mr Jones) the headmaster for crossing the line separating the playgrounds and kissing Tina Griffiths. It was probably a dare, but from the head's point of view I really had 'crossed the line'.

When my parents were informed of my totally unacceptable behaviour, they just laughed! It was here I had my first crush, Claire Humphries. She was olive-skinned, dark-eyed and dark-haired, and I was gutted when her family moved their jewellery shop up north somewhere. But all of us boys had a crush on Miss Williams our class teacher. She must have been in her early twenties, just out of teaching college, and in her 'flower power' garb seemed like a breath of fresh air compared to the older teachers. She read the *Chronicles of Narnia* out loud to us and I remember being enthralled by the fantasy worlds and characters of C. S. Lewis's imagination. Miss Williams admitted to us that she had a crush on footballer Geoff Hurst (West Ham and England), we all thought he was pretty cool too, but Manchester United player Georgie Best was the best as far as we were concerned! A fabulously skilled football player and sporting superstar.

Morning assemblies were quite formal. We sat cross-legged on the thickly varnished wooden floorboards in the main hall like generations of border-country kids before us. Huge song sheets were hung on the wall (like hymns in a church) and we would all sing from these, a different song each day. I particularly remember 'Glad That I Live am I' and can still remember some of the words, as the description of the countryside resonated with me:

Glad that I live am I, That the sky is blue, Glad for the country lanes and the fall of dew, After the sun the rain, After the rain the sun, This is the way of life 'til our work be done. The last bit certainly sounds rather Victorian, if not Orwellian.

If we were very lucky a huge, wooden cabinet carrying a black-and-white television on a tall, shiny pole was occasionally wheeled into the hall and we were allowed to watch *Picture Box* presented by Joan Bakewell.

We had one nature visit (to Cae Glas Park across the road) and had to collect autumn leaves to draw and colour-in.

I suppose that my appreciation of art started here though, because in the hall hung a Lowry picture with its matchstick men and matchstick cats and dogs with smoke pouring out of the factory chimneys in an industrial landscape. I loved its naive, childlike style and would often lose myself in it.

From The National School I attended Oswestry Grammar (founded in 1407); I still have my silver cap badge. P. S. Jones was our PE teacher, always dressed in his tracksuit with a whistle hung around his neck (to give the impression he was athletic and actually working). He would generally send us on a cross-country run around 'the triangle'. If one of us happened to be off games he would send us down to the corner shop to get a bottle of cellophane-wrapped Lucozade and packet of cigarettes – a wonderful demonstration of a supposedly healthy lifestyle!

From here I briefly attended Priory Grammar School for Boys in Shrewsbury. I can't quite believe it, but I studied Latin and Ancient Greek! It was there that I first met Dewi, both of us being put in detention on my first day of attendance by 'Rubberneck', the physics teacher, for talking in class. We both ended up in the choir singing 'Zadok the Priest' in St Chad's Church at Christmas. We were keen participants as we were allowed to miss maths lessons for rehearsals and were given Mars Bars as an extra incentive. The choirmaster was obviously having to scrape the barrel for willing choristers. It may also explain why we are both so terrible at maths!

My mother, a talented watercolour artist, has massively influenced my love of art, mainly through the beautifully illustrated sketchbooks she has produced over the last few decades. She has undoubtedly had a huge influence on the whole family, and two generations have gone on to pursue careers in art or design. My brother Mike's sketchbooks are charming and humorous. Most are travel diaries which began life as we explored rural France in the first few years after my father's death.

My mother had a white Daihatsu jeep, and she would hire a caravan for two or three weeks each summer holiday which we would tow around the minor D roads of France. We didn't really have a particular destination; these were 'road trips' and we just went where the old *Quiet Roads of France* book led us. There were huge distances; it took a while to get used to the scale of the map and size of the country. We travelled along straight, tree-shaded roads with occasional groups of smiling, tanned cyclists and passed sunny, bright, 'Impressionist landscapes' of golden sunflowers and scented, purple lavender, walnut groves, wide sparkling rivers and through extensive, well-managed oak forests.

Exotic lizards sunned themselves on warm, ancient walls. We passed mistletoe-clothed orchards grazed by old-fashioned-looking cattle and sleepy farmyards with neatly stacked log piles, vintage machinery and old rusting cars. It was like stepping back in time (probably how England used to be, I thought, but now mostly gone or tidied up). We drove through breath-taking mountain scenery in the Jura, the winding gorge roads between Annecy and Grenoble, the eerie solitude and quiet emptiness of the Massif Central. A country so close to home, yet so interestingly different and unspoilt.

On a couple of occasions, we took Dewi and John Morris with us – how we all fitted into the jeep and caravan I will never know! Those trips were fun. We gorged ourselves on Nutella and baguettes, smoked Gauloises (*sans-filtre bien sûr*) from the Tabac, picked wild strawberries to have with our muesli, got sozzled on white wine and cheese fondues, added Cassis to cheap *vin blanc*, ended up driving the wrong way down narrow, cobbled streets and once inadvertently drove straight through the middle of a very serious-looking boules contest in a gravelled village square!

I can still picture the lovely, winding D996 between Dijon and Dole, the visit to Louis Pasteur's house, seeing the Bayeux Tapestry for real (not in a book), being blown away by the magnificent stained-glass windows in Chartres Cathedral, the Roman amphitheatre at Nîmes, the medieval town of Carcassonne, the first sight of Mont St Michel appearing through the coastal mist and being humbled into silence by the stark rows of mass war graves in Normandy, things my mother had wanted us to experience. In later years she let slip that she had taken out personal bank loans to ensure we got a proper summer holiday.

I am eternally grateful to her for introducing us to this beautiful country, for sharing her sense of adventure – and for her presumably great patience! Consequently, I think we are all Francophiles. My first car was a rather utilitarian 1969

Renault 4 van (£150) with bench seat, gear stick in the dash and F sticker proudly displayed on the back. I must have seemed a bit of a prat as a sixth former: I wore a striped Breton shirt, red Kicker boots and undoubtedly bounced around to Plastique Bertrand's 'Ca Plane Pour Moi'. (None of us, perhaps unsurprisingly, voted for Brexit).

We once visited my father's old boss Ian Beer and family in Sussex. He had been the headmaster of Ellesmere College during my father's time teaching there and had taken over the rather prestigious job of head of Lancing College (and later Harrow). We drove down in my father's old Jaguar (maroon coloured, with cream leather seats and wire-spoked wheels) and I remember being rather overawed by the majesty of the place – could this really be a school? While there we went to Billy Smart's Circus (probably in Worthing). It was exciting initially but turned into a bit of a nightmare for me. When the much-awaited clowns came on to perform, they asked if any child would like to join them for some fun and I naively raised my hand. My memory may be slightly blurred with the effects of PTSD, but I recall being placed on a chair and beaten with pretend truncheons in front of a laughing audience. It was humiliating; I think I cried. Funnily enough I have hated clowns ever since!

We also visited the Dolphinarium in Brighton, which turned out to be another rather traumatic event. Mike smashed his head against a glass window of the aquarium in the café and the pane fell out onto the table – no injuries luckily – but for a moment we all thought the dolphins were going to join us for afternoon tea! Sometime after this I had to go to the dentist to have some crowded teeth removed. I was given gas and can still remember the flickering image of the Venetian blinds as I went under. In my gas-induced dream my mouth had become a circus big top; a huge, red, timber support pole came loose and started knocking the giant white tent down, pole by pole, section by section… the teeth in my mouth being pulled out one by one. I think I know where the big-top nightmare had come from.

Through our early teens our friends were mainly farmers' kids, and their farms were our adventure playgrounds. Here we created labyrinths of tight tunnels in hay or straw barns, with dark pit traps to fall into – how we have all survived I will never know!

The farms were dangerous places and both Mikes (brother and cousin) ended up in A&E with broken limbs from falling out of barns. There were drums of fuel, oil and chemicals and piles of old agricultural equipment rusting amongst clumps of nettles, old tractors and combine harvesters to clamber over, there were rat holes everywhere… it was in these exciting, dangerous places that we spent much of our free time.

One particular activity comes back to me; being towed at frightening speed around the lower slopes of Sweeney Mountain behind a tractor on 'Big Bertha'. Big Bertha was the remaining axles and frame of an old stock-feeding trough; its wheels were cast iron and we sat perched along its heavy timber beam. Mark Edwards ('Spud') would tear around the fields with all of us clinging on for dear life. On one painfully memorable occasion, when I was seated at the front, we careered over a tree sapling which sprang up and whacked me in the testicles! In winter when the fields were covered in snow, we tied shovels to the back of the tractor or Land Rover and 'snow surfed' on them, holding onto the wooden shafts and regularly falling off in fits of uncontrollable laughter.

We occasionally earned a bit of pocket money picking potatoes. This was horrible work; cold and wet and being harassed by Spud coming up behind us on the tractor to hurry us up and collect our heavy sacks. At £3.50 a day it soon lost its attraction. However, delivering the potatoes was more enjoyable, but no pay. We would lie on top of a whole load of potato sacks piled high in the back of Mr Edwards's grossly overloaded Land Rover and deliver potatoes around the Welsh Border country southwest of Oswestry – aah, the 'health-and-safety-free' seventies!

Even at this young age we were sometimes pretty alarmed by some of the damage we saw being done to the environment; this was a time of serious grubbing out of hedges, small gateways being bulldozed into bigger ones and all kinds of rubbish pushed over banks out of sight. I can remember all too well the harrowing discovery of numerous piglet remains spread across a large, recently muck-sprayed field next to a pig farm. Dewi's younger brother John was so annoyed and upset at seeing the destruction a bulldozer had been doing to some woodland that he simply took away the key... early eco warriors!

During our teens, after we lost Dad, my brothers and I were very fortunate in attending Ellesmere College, benefiting from a private school education. This privilege (perhaps not hugely recognised by us at the time but appreciated now) was down to the generosity of the headmaster (who gifted us a complimentary education) and some generous family friends who helped contribute.

I can remember my first day, sitting at a long-benched table in the dining hall at lunchtime, with our house prefect M. P. Davies at the top end. 'More water Russell, get another jug!' he ordered me. 'Get it yourself. Who do you think you are, the bloody King?' I angrily replied. There was a deadly hush as I slid the empty jug back down the table. He ordered me to clean his rugby boots later as a punishment. I just wiped spit on them.

I quickly realised that I wasn't going to fit easily into this place, full of toffs, testing traditions and ridiculous rules. It is interesting to note that when my father first started teaching at Ellesmere, prefects were still administering corporal punishment. However, Ian Beer (the new headmaster – and still only in his twenties) soon put a stop to that, despite a threatened mutiny from prefects and some of the more traditionally entrenched schoolmasters.

In a geography lesson one day Mr Newbold asked everyone what newspapers their families usually had delivered. *The Telegraph* and *Financial Times* seemed to be top of the list, and when it came my turn, I naively said, '*The Shropshire Star.*' There were sniggers from the other pupils – I didn't quite understand why at the time (and we didn't have it delivered – we had to go and get it ourselves).

For a homework project we were asked to design a new town. I based mine on a cartwheel design and painstakingly coloured-in the broad, spoked green corridors of woodlands and recreational areas. I called the town 'Llareggub', which resulted in a lot of red-penned comments and exclamation marks! I guess that served me right really for plagiarising Dylan Thomas and trying to be smart. I suppose that I should have been more grateful for the privileged education that Ellesmere College provided me. I left with nine 'O' Levels but didn't want to stay on after that – it wasn't for me.

Ellesmere College is a magnificent red-brick, rather Gothic building, with resident rooks constantly calling from the ancient rookery in its Scots pines. Due to this atmospheric appearance, it was chosen as the fictional Catholic school St Anthony's in the film *Absolution*, starring Richard Burton and Billy Connolly and directed by Anthony Page (I expect he named the school after himself). A huge film crew and actors descended on the school during spring 1978, turning much of it into a film set. This was wonderfully distracting for us pupils and we were fascinated to watch how a movie was made, but probably even more impressed by the cameraman's overly emblazoned Pontiac Firebird with huge golden eagle on the bonnet – and Richard Burton's rather stunning wife!

Many of us were used as extras and I was lucky enough to be chosen to be Dai Bradley's 'stand in' and had 'to die' in a swimming pool scene. Dai Bradley was the actor who played Billy in Ken Loach's acclaimed film *Kes*. Having had a kestrel myself for a while I identified with Billy, and we had recently studied the book *A Kestrel for a Knave* in our English class. It was a fascinating few weeks and my mother says she will never forget me introducing her to Richard Burton. He signed our old LP recording of him narrating *Under Milk Wood* and scribbled 'Break a Leg!' on the underside of my skateboard.

We were all keen skateboarders and would spend hours and hours riding the winding hill roads or honing our skills on the plywood quarter-pipe we had on the drive. Amazingly, I managed to persuade the games master to let us have skateboarding as a recognised sport – thereafter a small team skateboarded on Wednesday afternoons instead of having to play rugby!

That must have been a first at a very traditional public school. I remember selling a beautiful old pot lid I had once dug up so that I could afford to buy a set of Kryptonic wheels (£26.50, so expensive at the time). All of us still bear scars from those skateboarding adventures and, perhaps rather stupidly, despite our ageing bodies we all still occasionally give it a go… but not too fast! As an 'old school' skater it is wonderful to see that it has now been recognised as an excellent activity for maintaining health and wellbeing in older years, has regained its grip on a new generation and is now an official Olympic sport.

I left Ellesmere College and went to the local technical college in Oswestry to do a National Diploma in Science. It was all so very different: we didn't have to wear uniforms, our lecturers treated us like adults, and we didn't have to call them 'Sir', but Dave, or Jim, or whatever their name was. Next door was a new leisure centre where we would go at breaks, have coffees, mix with loads of other students, smoke, play Space Invaders and put UB40 or The Jam on the jukebox. Our course had fewer than ten participants, so we had an excellent teacher-to-student ratio.

We had an eclectic mix of students, from very different backgrounds, all real characters. Geraint, very shy and quiet, travelled in from the depths of mid Wales. Barry still thought it was 1974 (so was at least four years behind the fashion scene), and wore huge-collared shirts, a tank top, platform shoes and Oxford bags. Gareth, very tall, bright and academic (from the high school), had a wonderful, curtained centre parting and played bass in a band. Robert, a very measured, mature student with mandatory dark brown corduroy jacket, travelled all the way from Telford on the bus. Kathy, with hairspray-fixed hair, a bit gobby and entertaining, refused to do any dissections. Christopher, another mature student, wore thick glasses, was incredibly conscientious and immaculately turned out with jacket, checked shirt and tie. Catherine always underestimated herself but worked hard and actually did very well. Steve, an old school friend from years ago, my main buddy on the course, smoked a lot and always wore a lumberjack jacket. And me, from the 'posh school'.

I majored in biology and chemistry. Jim Durston was our biology lecturer and did his best to keep us focused on the subject, which thankfully, most of the time he did.

He was a gentle giant, with a mass of tangled dark curly hair and beard, a blue Guernsey jumper (usually covered in chalk) under a brown corduroy jacket (whatever the weather), flared Levi jeans and Nature Trek shoes. He would lollop into our class like a great big bear (usually a little late) and attempt to get order by immediately, and quite illegibly, scratching the lesson's topic on the blackboard. He had a bulging, battered briefcase, which he could never close, its handle held together with old electrical wires. We used to wind him up a lot, but we had great respect for him; he made biology fun and was an excellent teacher. I owe a lot to Jim's patience with me.

Occasionally we would escape the confines of the biology lab and Jim would take us pond dipping and ecological surveying, squashed into the back of his canvas-topped ex-military Land Rover. Every now and then we'd meet him in his local pub for a pint. He never seemed to be with anyone else; I think he was quite lonely really.

Dave Barker was our physics teacher. He had a broad Yorkshire accent, loved his real ale and was a chain smoker. He would kindly share his strong, filter-less Gold Leaf cigarettes with Steve and I and took us all potholing in the Peak District. I'm not entirely sure what that had to do with our physics curriculum, but it was quite an adventure – and one of my scariest experiences!

Oswestry Tech was a very different world from Ellesmere College, and I loved it. I was the entertainments organiser for the Students Union and occasionally organised disco parties at Morton Lodge with a hired coach laid on for transport.

I was really happy there – it was a wonderful, carefree couple of years. I learned and laughed at the same time.

It was while I was there that I had my first proper girlfriend, Bryony Blase (great name). She later left me to go out with Steve!

I can remember being impressed with some of Steve's stuff when we were nine or ten, kids of the exciting and all-consuming 'Space Age'. He undoubtedly had Oswestry's first Raleigh Chopper (yellow), the first proper skateboard I'd ever seen (brought over from America) with smooth Cadillac wheels, a shiny white telescope with tripod (the only kid we knew with one) for looking at the moon, and a two-foot-high model of the Apollo 11 Saturn Five rocket... cool stuff indeed!

In the two or three years before the alehouses of Oswestry got their smoky claws into us, our winter evenings would be spent watching TV. Much of it was American, mainly cops and detectives: *Starsky and Hutch*, *Columbo*, *Ironside* and *Frank Cannon PI*. Lots of shooting and car chases, tyres squealing in parking lots, bins and boxes being smashed through in back-street alleys, oversized gas guzzlers and giant trucks bashing each other off dusty desert highways.

Occasionally we would go to the rather spartan Regal cinema (with its sewn-patched screen) and watch films such as

Smokey and The Bandit, *The Gumball Rally* and *Convoy*. I saw my first X-rated film here with Dewi: *Easy Rider* (a drug-induced motorbike adventure following Route 66), starring Peter Fonda and Dennis Hopper. We were probably more familiar with Californian landscapes and the streets of LA and New York than we were of our own country and cities.

I will never forget the opening scene of the first *Star Wars* movie in 1977 as the lines of yellow writing gradually disappeared into the dark depths of distant space and the largest spaceship imaginable passed over the top of us. You could feel its vibration shaking the poor-quality and ageing cinema sound system to its limits.

Devil's Rocks was very close to our house: the remains of an old quarry with its own pond, cave and wonderful, giant rounded-boulder cliffs. A more 'Stig of the Dump' like place would be hard to find. The sandstone quarry must have been worked a couple of hundred years previously because it was now wooded, and the pond (with cliff-side cave) was as natural and prehistoric as any child could imagine. If I think about it, I can still recall the smell of coconut-scented gorse above the rocks and the heavy scent of wild mint down by the pool. Running back home we would kick dried-out molehills to make them 'explode' like the landmines in the finishing credits of the *Dad's Army* TV series. When I was about nine or ten, I entered a national poetry competition and wrote a poem about Devil's Rocks which, to my surprise (and delight) I won, and I received an olive-coloured PaperMate biro in a see-through plastic box as a prize!

We visited this magical place well into our late teens, when we would sit around a campfire late into the night above the huge sandstone boulders on the cliff top swigging beer, smoking roll-ups, feeling free and unshackled. However, we all sadly knew that these days wouldn't last forever, and that the wider world would eventually pull us away and apart, which of course it inevitably did.

I will never forget that Sweeney Mountain childhood. Cousins growing up so near to each other, closely bonded by the shared loss of much-loved fathers, keeping ourselves occupied, distracting ourselves from the elephant in the room – our underlying repressed shock and trauma. We did our best to enjoy ourselves and to try and make some sense of it all, to come to terms with and to accept life's cruel throw of the dice. Our family homes separated by a little wood on top of a hill, each adventurous and carefree day just merging into the next.

We were starting to leave our childhoods and the 1970s behind (flared trousers, discos, punk, vinyl LPs, Chopper bikes and Ford Capris) and sliding into a new decade of Thatcher, austerity, beige Mini Metros, shiny CDs, the Cold War, the Falklands War, miners' strikes, 'Hooray Henrys' with wide red braces... and becoming students.

Having obtained an OND certificate in Science I was accepted on an Environmental Biology degree course at Oxford ... Polytechnic. Having never lived in a city before, I found Oxford to be both charming and contradictory.

Privilege and poverty well used to scraping uncomfortably alongside each other for centuries; the extremes of Town and Gown came as quite a shock to a country boy. Cowley Road formed the main corridor or portal between these two completely different worlds. At its western end rose the dreaming, honey-coloured medieval spires of privileged academia, while at its eastern end were sprawling housing estates and noisy car factories. Parallel universes, not too unlike Lyra's Oxford in Philip Pullman's *His Dark Materials.*

Oxford was, however, and perhaps unsurprisingly, a splendid place to be a student. Here I met some of my life-long friends, shared a grotty house with a fun-bunch of rural estate management undergraduates, a freezing flat above a hairdresser's salon and got to know some splendid old pubs: The Turf Tavern, The Perch, The Bear and The Bullingdon Arms to name a few. In The Eagle and Child it felt a privilege to be drinking in the same pub where the Inklings (a literary society including J. R. R. Tolkien and C. S. Lewis) met each week to discuss their works in progress. Sitting in the same spot where the magical worlds of Middle Earth and Narnia were conceived and discussed, you could almost smell the pipe smoke!

While I was at Oxford my mother announced that she was getting remarried. My siblings and I now had a stepbrother John and stepsister Emma, who both coincidently studied their degrees at the university and polytechnic too.

Gaining an environmental biology degree from the polytechnic led to my first job as Assistant Nature Reserve

Officer at Slapton Ley National Nature Reserve in the summer of 1984 working for the Field Studies Council in Devon: the start of my career in countryside management.

Chapter Three: A Fortunate Place

Slapton is a very special place – in fact *A Fortunate Place*, as described by Robin Stanes in his comprehensive history of the settlement. It is a pretty, ancient village tucked away in the gentle folds of the South Devon countryside half a mile inland (and protectively hidden) from the sea. Many people will no doubt remember staying at the Field Studies Centre on a residential field trip with their school or college. Between the village and the sea is a nationally important nature reserve of shingle beach, reed beds, freshwater lake, marsh and ancient woodland. A road, known locally as The Line, runs along the ridge of the beach between Torcross and Strete Gate and the area is extremely popular with holidaymakers and naturalists. A beautiful stretch of blue sea and golden beach in summer and dark, swirling clouds of starlings over the bare, straw-coloured reed beds in winter. What better place to begin a career in countryside conservation?

Working for the FSC was the perfect transition between being a student and the real world, a halfway house where I still felt free of most of life's responsibilities and stresses yet also 'grown-up' and employed. Not only that, but my job included full board and lodging and the field centre's infamous afternoon tea and cake served at 4 o'clock! 'Proper job' as Arthur Bowles, the cheery gardener, would often say.

During the summer holidays, when schools and colleges were closed, the field centre offered residential and daily courses to the public. These were popular with families with bored teenagers stuck for things to do, and holidaymakers looking for something to entertain themselves on a wet August day when sitting on the beach was not that appealing.

It was on one of these visits that I was first properly introduced to this very special little corner of England. In the hot summer of 1976, the year after Dad died, my mother took us to stay at Slapton on a family residential course – 'Exploring South Devon'. What else was she going to do with three lost boys? We were introduced to this fascinating area: the rugged cliffs and white-washed lighthouse at Start Point, the ruined fishing village of Hallsands and its tragic story of destruction, evening rowing-boat trips on the lake, a visit to atmospheric Wistman's Wood on Dartmoor, rock pooling at East Prawle, looking at brightly coloured lichens through microscopes, badger watching in Slapton Wood and of course, ice cream or fish n' chip treats at Torcross. My first ever sneaky cigarette. We loved it.

So, starting a job at Slapton was not too daunting for me and I was excited to have the chance to live and work in this rather enchanting place. A couple of months before finishing my degree in Oxford I had written to Keith Chell, the Warden of the Field Studies Centre, to explain that I was just about to finish my environmental biology degree – I wondered if he might have some work for me? I had often thought that a field centre ecology tutor would be a great job, but anything would be good really. I had known Keith a few years before, when he was at Preston Montford. I worked a summer there when I finished college (as handyman and gardener) and had come to know him pretty well, but more to the point, he knew me. I had recently stayed at the centre on a residential field trip as part of my degree course, studying the ecology of the shingle ridge, freshwater lake, woodland and coastal habitats, but in a much more detailed manner than during my holiday stay back in 1976!

I half expected a reply along the lines of, 'Hi Tim, nice to hear from you, but sorry nothing available at the moment. Good luck with the job hunting,' but instead he replied with, 'Hi Tim, nice to hear from you. What good timing, we were just about to advertise the post of Assistant Nature Reserve Officer, would you like the job?'

I couldn't quite believe it! I had my first job in conservation lined up with full board and lodging in sunny South Devon. I hadn't even finished my degree and working on the nature reserve sounded much more fun than actually being a tutor! I guess it's down to who you know sometimes... and this was an opportunity not to be missed. I didn't feel too guilty as getting that first job in conservation is notoriously difficult. Employers don't want to give you a job unless you have relevant experience, but you can't get experience unless someone gives you a job. The usual 'way in' is to do a couple of years' volunteering – so this was a real chance to get my foot in the door. During my first week or two Tony Thomas, who had been the previous Warden (and was now Director of the Field Studies Council), came to Slapton for a visit, and he came up to say hello and to congratulate me on the job. 'People usually go on to great things after working here,' he said. It felt far too early to even think about 'what next', but at least it seemed that Slapton was going to give me a good grounding for the future.

On my first day at work, a glorious sunny day in early August, I was told that in a couple of days I was to lead the 'Flowers of the Shingle Ridge' walk for the public as a part of the summer season of family guided walks and talks. I rather reluctantly spent the next two days cooped up in the tiny, damp and sunless library swotting up on my botany. I felt a bit thrown in at the deep end, but soon became rather enthralled by yellow-horned poppy and viper's bugloss! Apparently, there were adders out on the coastal heath too, and I was extremely keen to find one.

I survived that first guided walk, very glad that I had done my homework. The twenty or so people attending seemed to enjoy it too, so as far as I was concerned it was a roaring success. I had also learned where to find adders on the sunny bank just above Slapton Bridge and everyone was impressed that these beautiful and exciting reptiles could be safely seen at close quarters. The next walk I had to lead was simply called 'An Introduction to Slapton Ley Nature Reserve' – a doddle compared to the previous botanically themed one (I thought). My route was around the shore of the lake (the pre-ice age coastline) and back to Slapton, not missing the adders along the way. Most people, I soon came to appreciate, had never seen an adder before, so being almost guaranteed to find them at the same spot was a great start.

Halfway through the walk, with an eclectic group of attendees, a father pointed into the sky and asked, 'What's that large bird up there?' This was going to be easy. 'A buzzard,' I said. I then tried to be too clever for my own good: '*Bufo bufo.*' 'I think you'll find that *Bufo bufo* is actually the common toad,' added an older gentleman in a floppy canvas hat, khaki shorts and carrying binoculars. I had meant to say *Buteo buteo*! I decided to steer clear of scientific Latin names after that. I gradually gained my confidence, however, and added more walks to my portfolio, leading evening walks around the village on the 'History of Slapton' (with a complimentary pint in the Tower Inn afterwards for bringing in a few customers), Rock Pool Safaris down at East Prawle and the iconic circular walk around Start Point, undoubtedly one of my favourites, with almost a guarantee of watching seals and sky-diving gannets. I was beginning to do the job I had always wanted to do, introducing people to nature, making it fun and really enjoying it myself.

I soon fell in love with Slapton, its field centre, village life and the surrounding South Hams countryside – it is difficult not to. A new experience for me was hearing the sonic boom created by Concorde as it hurtled overhead at twice the speed of sound just before 11.00 am each morning on its regular flight to New York, rattling the sash windows and quite usefully announcing coffee break! A sound almost forgotten now and unlikely to be heard again. Even then, back in the mid-eighties, this seemed a rather indulgent flight for the super-rich and a throwback to the gas-guzzling seventies.

Being out in the nature reserve most days was a privilege. New sights and sounds filled my senses: huge hornets in the dead elms, Cetti's warblers, water rail and a bittern in the reed beds, murmurations of wheeling starlings and circling buzzards overhead. The mild climate and soft sea air were different from what I was used to and initially I found that I was constantly tired, but the clean coastal air, hard physical work and lots of walking soon began to do a rather unfit ex-student the world of good. I was in my element.

One of my roles was Beach Warden, and this element of the job was funded through the local council and came with its own official ID badge. I would mainly be advising the public about the area, checking on inappropriate car parking, dealing with illegal camping and fires, litter picking and patrolling The Line in the nature reserve's Subaru pick-up. Even then, back in 1984, I was shocked at the amount of plastic washed up on the beach, some of it from far-flung places so I assumed it had literally been dumped overboard.

I can remember feeling slightly guilty as I woke up on a bright, sunny morning with my litter picker and rubbish bag next to me, having dozed off listening to the very relaxing shhhh, shhhh sound of the sea dragging shingle as each wave retreated. On a still night this wonderfully soporific and soothing sound could sometimes be heard in the village and would gently lull me to sleep.

This shingle proved to be a very valuable component in the huge extensions to Devonport dockyards during the First World War, but its controversial dredging from Start Bay and the subsequent destruction of Hallsands village is a perfect environmental lesson for us still, over one hundred years later. A massive 650,000 tons of shingle were taken from the bay to add to the concrete mix; it was cheap, there seemed to be a lot of it and it was close to Plymouth. However, this shingle was the result of a one-off 'fossil' event, pushed from forty miles away by rising sea levels following the last ice age.

The Government and Navy were warned by locals and scientists that removal of this huge amount of shingle would cause the beach levels to drop and the protective beach widths to narrow. This happened – and is still happening. The shingle that had protected the coast for thousands of years was no longer there, and Hallsands village was washed away. Hard sea defences (unlike the natural soft shingle one) have had to be built to protect villages such as Torcross and the main road, and the future survival of Slapton Ley, the southwest's largest natural lake, is in doubt.

A great example of not messing with the environment unless you fully understand the consequences.

One of my main projects was to repair and improve the very popular but rather tired and deteriorating nature trail that wound its way from Slapton Bridge around the shores of the lake. This was enjoyable and rewarding work and the addition of a new boardwalk section through the reed beds added a whole new experience and created an alternative, longer footpath link back to the village.

Getting the supporting wooden pallets tanalised was quite memorable; this was done at a timber yard in Newton Abbot. I got the heavily laden Luton van embarrassingly wedged tight in the mainline railway tunnel, holding up traffic in both directions. It starts off square and quite normal but (unbeknown to me) very quickly reverts to the lower Victorian arched version. I had to let all the tyres down to rather sheepishly reverse out, the roof of the van looking like a partly opened sardine tin. Recently, I came through the tunnel for the first time since then while taking my stepson Ben for a driving lesson. He smiled wryly when I told him the story and the fact that prior to getting stuck I had just had a lunchtime pint in the quite aptly named Devon Dumpling – after all, I felt like one! A driving lesson for us all.

The winter storms of 1984–85 had brought some huge trees down in Slapton Wood. Some of these could lie where they fell to slowly rot away as a vital part of the natural woodland cycle. Large rotting trees, fallen or standing, would have been commonplace in our ancient forests, but are now quite rare.

Others had fallen across the main circular trail within the wood and their impassable trunks needed to be cut through or their tangle of blocking branches cleared. I was sent on a chainsaw course. It was on our initial clearing mission that I soon learnt how to respect the hidden dangers when dealing with a fallen tree and to appreciate at first-hand why thorough chainsaw training was so important.

Simon and I loaded the Subaru pick-up with the saws, fuel, first-aid kit and packed lunch and drove up the old sunken track to the top of the wood. It was a case of walking and carrying after that. We eventually reached the large ash tree that had fallen across the path. It faced uphill, and you could have just about squeezed underneath its massive bulk. Simon carefully assessed the tree to establish how much tension lay in its mighty trunk by creating a series of shallow vertical cuts a few inches apart.

Windblown trees are notorious for holding powerful, unleashed, twisted tension just waiting to explode. All seemed OK. He nodded towards me, indicating that he was going to start his first proper cut. He let the chainsaw sink a few inches deeper. Without warning, the huge bole cracked with an almighty snap and sprang sideways and upwards into the air, throwing Simon with it and missing his face by inches. He was rightly shaken; it could easily have killed him! We calmed our nerves with a swig of tea and discussed the next move. Now that the tree's tension had been released, we were able to cut a section wide enough for people to walk through, but not without hitting some metal in the tree first.

Many of the old trees in the wood have shrapnel and bullets buried in their trunks, war wounds from the D-Day landing practice exercises held on Slapton Beach. This was the main reason why the wood had survived any post-war felling: the shrapnel had made the timber too difficult to mill and sell. Its war wounds were its saviour.

Those couple of winters that brought the trees down were also incredibly cold. The Lower Ley actually froze over, a rare sight indeed for such a large body of water in one of the most southerly parts of the country, literally yards from the sea. Swans that were used to landing gracefully on smooth, forgiving water slid unexpectedly, ungracefully and quite comically across the ice, ending up in rather confused crumpled heaps. Their freshwater food source was unavailable to them, so we fed them with hay for a while down near the sluice gate in Torcross. Thousands of starlings congregated in the sky above the reed beds each afternoon, returning from desperate feeding forays and landing to roost amongst the shelter of the reeds as one dark mass with a loud 'whoosh' just as the weak, winter light was fading.

The surrounding countryside lay stunningly white under a blanket of snow, highlighting its undulating character, a dazzling contrast with the flat expanse of brilliant blue sea. Sunken lanes were full of snow drifts and my fiancée Jill and I were the last people to get to Slapton down Five Mile Lane one very snowy night. The lane has high hedges, is deeply cut and winding and has some very exposed ridges. Snow had blown through some of the field gates forming deep drifts across the lane, well over the height of the Subaru. I literally had to punch the vehicle through these at full pelt, headlights illuminating a dense white wall; at times the four wheels were literally swimming through the snow until finding some bite on the tarmac again. It was a memorable journey, but we got through. There could have been a very different end to the evening – there were no mobile phones in those days.

Living and breathing Slapton's slow pace of life and calming environment allowed me to let myself go, to unwind and really appreciate what the natural world can do for one's imagination and well-being if you just spend some time in it and let it in. One beautiful spring day out in the reserve I stopped for a break and lay on my back in the sun on the side of a grassy hill overlooking the sparkling freshwater lake and shimmering sea. With arms and legs outstretched, I stared into the sky and gazed past the fluffy white clouds into the deeper blue beyond. It was like looking down into forever. 'It's a good job we've got gravity,' I thought, 'otherwise I would just free-fall into space.'

It had never really crossed my mind before that because the world is a sphere, just spinning in space, there is no real up or down. When we look up into the sky, we are also looking down into the deepest pool imaginable. It was a bit of a revelation and I still love that sensation.

One late autumn afternoon, after a stroll through Slapton Wood which ended up on the beach near Strete Gate, I lay on the cool golden shingle and gazed into the darkening steely sky. A single trail of long, lumpy grey clouds began to develop over the sea and move towards me. The setting sun caught their western flanks, and they became more rounded and three-dimensional. As I lay on the shingle, I imagined that I was lying on the seabed looking up through the water as a family of whales passed above me. Once again, I was captivated by nature's beauty; the simple event of some clouds passing over me enabled my imagination to run free.

Allowing yourself to become completely absorbed in nature is one of life's true pleasures. Unfortunately, we rarely give ourselves time to do this in our busy, hectic lives, but I know that it has often 'saved me' in difficult times. In a recent conversation my partner Victoria, explained how she loved exploring around her childhood farm in Bantham, but dreaded having to go indoors at dusk as she wanted to enjoy being a part of that twilight world with the animals she loved. This feeling has stayed with her ever since and still inspires her as an artist and illustrator to this day.

Once, my cousin Mike Harold came to visit. He had spent some time travelling and then working in the Royal Chitwan National Park in northern India. I wanted to show him some of my local wild places, so I took him to Dartmoor. There is a wonderful walk down the east side of the River Dart from Dartmeet that takes you through ancient, mossy woodland to some waterfalls and rocky platforms where you can sit in the middle of the river surrounded by steep wooded slopes, the perfect place to get away from people and back to nature. We sat on the rock slabs, poured a coffee each from the flask, grabbed a sarnie and gazed down the wild river valley. The only sound came from the rushing water and the wind in the trees. 'Not a bad spot, is it?' I said.

Before he had time to reply, a deep, repetitive throbbing sound become apparent and grew louder by the second, reverberating up the narrow valley. We couldn't see where it was coming from at first, but suddenly, flying just above the water around a bend in the river, two huge Chinook helicopters headed directly over the top of us. It was like some bizarre alien invasion: they seemed completely out of place, a scene from *Apocalypse Now*. My magic 'wild spot' was literally blown out of the water. 'Nowhere is truly wild in England anymore,' I sadly thought to myself.

I eventually convinced my friend Dewi to come and work at Slapton. A new job managing a Manpower Services Commission (MSC) team had become available through Devon County Council and hosted by the field centre, and he got it. This meant carrying out land management projects on the nature reserve such as fencing, step building and tree planting. It was great to have my 'old mate' joining me down in sunny South Devon.

We were both keen to get involved with as much conservation and research work as we could and assisted Rob Poole (Pooey) with his oil pollution research work in the reed beds. Rob had devised a system of freeze-core extraction of reed rhizomes to assess the effects of oil pollution. Slapton's reed beds were clean and were used to compare oil-polluted sites next to Llandarcy Oil Refinery in South Wales. Unfortunately, this hard, unpleasant and tiring work. We had to carry the heavy scaffold poles and frozen cores (hand-winched from the mud) through the swampy reed beds, often sinking up to our waists. On the stinking, polluted Welsh site, in the humid heat of high summer we boiled in our boiler suits and were bitten to death by mosquitoes! We all shared an awful room in what must have been the cheapest B&B in Neath and had to literally 'break in' to Dale Fort Field Centre in the middle of the night (as Rob hadn't forewarned anyone of our arrival).

We returned to Slapton filthy and exhausted and didn't volunteer our services again after that! Rob went on to help Tim Smit discover the Lost Gardens of Heligan and then run Newquay Zoo.

I sometimes helped take groups from the field centre up onto Dartmoor, exploring Wistman's Wood (a small remnant of the native wildwood), learning about granite tor formation millions of years ago and assisting with river studies at Dartmeet. If we knew a field centre minibus was going to the moor on one of our days off Dewi and I would sometimes hitch a ride and get out for a good ramble over the moors.

Dartmoor is a truly magical place: its evocative landscapes, nature and depth of history pull you in. It is southern England's last really wild area and I fell in love with it too. I had missed my beloved Shropshire hill country while living in Oxford as a student, but here were rugged hills, wooded valleys, rushing rivers and expanses of untamed countryside which made me feel right at home.

In the autumn of 1985 on one of my first visits to Wistman's Wood I collected a couple of pocketsful of acorns. I didn't feel too guilty as I picked them off the ground from outside the experimental exclosure and they would have most likely been quickly eaten by sheep as succulent seedlings (oak regeneration is a real problem here due to grazing). I planted the acorns out in neat rows back at the field centre. A few years later, on a return visit I decided to see how they were doing, they were all about two to three feet tall and doing well.

I hope that they were planted somewhere out on the nature reserve; they would be over thirty years old now, about a tenth of the age of an oak tree in its prime. They have many, many decades left to thrive, absorbing carbon dioxide and giving out oxygen, in that very Fortunate Place.

However, after two years of 'living the dream' on very little pay I knew that I needed a proper salary and to make the next step in my career as I was now newly married. I had a great job, there was no doubt about it, but my prospects were limited. Simon, the Reserve Officer, seemed well entrenched – he wasn't going anywhere in a hurry.

A job came up as Assistant Countryside Officer for Oxford City Council, with a salary and house! I applied, had an interview up in Oxford and was offered the job.

Leaving Slapton would be one of the most difficult decisions I'd had to make in my life so far. I drove my old Morris Minor up to Start Point car park and slowly brought it to a spluttering stop, its rounded grey nose pointing out across the beautiful sweep of Start Bay below me. With arms resting on the steering wheel and a lot of sighing I gazed out over the sparkling sea to the yellow shingle beaches and distant green headlands. How could I leave this stunning place? I was beginning to feel that I really fitted in here. Should I just be patient and wait to see if Simon gets a job somewhere else? I knew that he had recently had an interview for the Warden's job on Lundy Island, I'd had my fingers crossed, but he decided not to take it.

He could be at Slapton for years; he really did have the perfect job – and two great village pubs to boot! It would have to be something very special indeed to pull him away – could I wait that long?

'OK,' I finally said to myself, 'I'll take the job, but I'll come back one day.'

Chapter Four: Spires and Sparrowhawks

A full-time, permanent job in conservation with a salary seemed quite an achievement at the age of twenty-five. I had only been out of college for two years and here I was back in Oxford with a responsible job with the City Council. It was also a great opportunity for my (then) wife Jill to do a postgraduate teaching course at our original polytechnic. During our time at Slapton we had both seen at first-hand how important education was in getting environmental messages across to people, particularly the next generation, and having a teaching certificate was an important stepping-stone to a job and career for her.

The house that came with the job was The Old Courthouse, the last remaining building of a long-gone medieval cluster of buildings called Bullingdon Green. Cavalry horses were stabled here during the Civil War. It was quite spooky, with inexplicable coughing often heard halfway up the stairs and metal rings still attached to its damp cellar walls, where unfortunate defendants were presumably held before trial.

We reached the house by driving down a long track between the tightly mown, manicured football pitches of Horspath municipal sports ground. Behind the house lay the dark and mysterious backdrop of Brasenose Wood and the rising hill of Shotover Country Park, the surviving remnant of an ancient hunting forest. My new boss, David Steel, had just written a book, *Shotover, The Natural History of a Royal Forest*, and he gave me a signed copy on my first day at work.

My official title was Assistant Countryside Officer; basically, I was the link between David (the Countryside Officer) and the ranger team, doing some of his work but mainly managing a rather eclectic bunch of Countryside Rangers. There was no vehicle for me initially, but David soon managed to get me one through the City's Parks Department. It was an old white Land Rover (OWL 248P) and had only been used for pulling grass cutters on school playing fields, occasionally pushing a snow plough and only had 20,000 miles on the clock. I soon came to love this little beast – it was wonderfully basic, had far too much play in the steering but surprisingly went like a rocket! This was quite handy when chasing illegal scramble bikes on the ancient trackway over the top of Shotover Plain.

This was the historic route from Oxford to London (the Old London Road) and was once notorious for highwaymen. Jackson's *Oxford Journal* reported on 12 January 1760:

Last Saturday Morning the Stagecoach was robbed about Five o'clock in the Morning at Shotover Hill, near this City, by two young Fellows in blue close-bodied Coats, mounted on black Horses; they took from the Passenger about seventeen Pounds, and after giving the Coachman and Postilion a Shilling each, rode off.

My Head Ranger (who wore a tight-fitting blue denim jacket with the sleeves cut off) was due to go on a residential basic ranger training course in the Peak District. Being an ex-shop steward from the nearby Cowley Motor Works he refused to go unless he got paid overtime for the extra 'travelling time' and evening sessions, so I jumped at the opportunity to take his place. A trip to the Peak District National Park, meeting other like-minded folk, sounded great. I had already heard tales of the infamous lock-ins in the bar at Losehill Hall Study Centre so headed north full of enthusiasm. I got some funny looks as I careered up the M6 in the old Land Rover which had 'Oxford City Council Has Dropped The Bomb' stickers emblazoned down its sides. Oxford was a Labour-run authority, and the stickers showed a number of snapped trident nuclear missiles in a dustbin!

I came back very inspired from the course and immediately set to smarten up my rangers and to install some much-needed professionalism. I ordered uniforms and badges and had Countryside Ranger lettering painted on our vehicles. At last, a smart and recognisable ranger service for the city. The Head Ranger somehow immediately 'lost' his new (and expensive, woollen) Barbour uniform jumper and 'accidently' power-washed the new signage and logos off his Land Rover... hmmm.

Having come from the Field Studies Council where all the staff conscientiously worked their socks off it was quite a shock working in a City Council, where there was a very different and entrenched work culture. Initially I found this extremely disappointing, frustrating and stressful, but decided to get on with the job and tried to enjoy it as much as I could.

I spent more of my time focusing on environmental education, bringing some of my experiences from Slapton, and joined forces with the local Wildlife Trust's Education Officer Fiona Danks, who was later to become a successful children's nature writer (with books including *The Stick Book* and *Nature's Playground*). In the summer holidays we provided a particularly valuable environmental playscheme, called Project Sparrowhawk. This ran for a whole week in Shotover Country Park and delivered environmentally themed activities for local families, including guided walks, nature-based games and lots of outdoor fun. It was hugely popular, totally exhausting for us, but a wonderful provision for the local community. It was quite an eye-opener for me in the different ways of engaging people in nature in a city environment, and the experience proved extremely useful when years later I was to become Plymouth's first urban ranger.

Below Shotover Hill, where the land flattens out, lies the ancient woodland of Brasenose Wood, a surviving remnant of Oxford's medieval past and once owned by Brasenose College.

My stepbrother John studied classics here, while I was at the polytechnic. I was invited to attend a dinner in the great dining hall; gowns were worn at top table and the Latin grace that we had reluctantly and robotically mumbled at Ellesmere College suddenly came in very handy. It was quite an experience; it now seems very 'Harry Potter' and was certainly very different from our noisy canteen up in Headington!

The college's unusual name is believed to come from a bronze door knocker that used to be on the main gate and is now mounted in the dining hall. According to legend, the knocker was created by Roger Bacon, the medieval thinker and Franciscan friar, whose quest for knowledge led him into alchemy and astrology and gave him the reputation of being something of a wizard. The knocker was supposedly created as a 'brazen head', a bronze head imbued with the power to speak and answer any question asked of it. Many mystics throughout history are said to have possessed similar items. According to the story, after creating the head Bacon gave the task of watching the head to his assistant Miles, who witnessed the head speak the words 'Time is' but didn't understand them so didn't alert his master. Half an hour later the head spoke the words 'Time was', to indicate that the time to question it had passed, before promptly bursting into flames. It is not known how Bacon reacted when Miles told him the news that his creation had worked, but he had missed it!

Brasenose Wood is situated just behind the house we lived in, and I would visit it often. It is designated as a Site of Special Scientific Interest, has a well-defined coppice-with-standards structure and is one of only a few ancient woodlands in the country that is still actively managed by this traditional method. The greater part of the wood is a remnant of the ancient hunting forest with a documented history dating back to the 13th century. It has a very diverse ground flora: 221 species of plants have been recorded, including 46 which are characteristic of ancient woodland. The rare black hairstreak butterfly is among the invertebrate inhabitants at the site due to plentiful blackthorn, which provides the main food source for the larvae. Many birds have been spotted within the wood, including tree pipit and grasshopper warbler.

One of my rangers was a keen birder, almost a twitcher. He was a biology graduate and was a little different from the rest of the team – he did things his own way. However, driving high-powered, expensive machinery was not exactly his forte. I can remember one snowy morning when he was using our huge four-wheel-drive tractor with a snow plough attachment, and I received a phone call: 'Tim, it's Rob, I've just driven the tractor into the back of a double-decker bus!' Good grief!

I headed off to Cowley Road, one of the main arteries into the city. A busier spot in Oxford at rush hour would be difficult to find! The tractor had literally 'ploughed' into the back of the bus, obliterated the rear engine and oil and water were spurting out all over the road. We somehow managed to placate some rather irate commuters and the bus driver, exchanged details and quickly made our departure.

I followed his 'driving' back to our works depot at Westhill Farm and as he turned into the narrow access lane, he obliviously scraped the plough and huge tyres down the side of a small car (with a rather shocked little old lady inside) and just carried on. Not long after this he ripped the sump off his new Land Rover on a tree stump. I could feel an additional staff training course was needed.

I can't complain too much, however, as I later got the front bumper of my Land Rover completely caught up in the brand-new chain-link fence that the allotment holders had just installed next to our offices at Brasenose Farm. Going forwards didn't help and reversing just messed it up even more, it was quite embarrassing, and the increasingly grumpy audience of headshaking, tut-tutting elderly men didn't really help! The vehicle became so entangled that I had to eventually cut it free with a pair of bolt croppers… they were not happy bunnies.

Every Friday I had to drive into Oxford city centre to drop off our time sheets and pick up the rangers' pay packets from the Town Hall. This seems incredibly old-fashioned now, but I used to love the opportunity to be by myself for a while and appreciate the splendour of this beautiful city. I never grew tired of driving the old Land Rover over Magdalen Bridge, past the tower and up the broad High Street to park in quiet, cobbled Merton Street and walk past Oriel College and Christchurch to the Town Hall. Oxford Town Hall's architecture is stunning both inside and out; it is the most amazing Gothic building and has been used in numerous films, including *Dracula*. After picking up the wage packets I would treat myself to a mid-morning break (a cheeseburger and coffee in nearby McDonalds) and embrace the heady freedom of being a boss – at least for half an hour or so!

I particularly enjoyed getting to know the rich array of riverside and wetland sites for which I was responsible, such as the beautiful Iffley Fritillary Meadows, historic Port Meadow and Aston's Eyot (eyot meaning 'island' in the Thames).

Walking along the quiet backwaters of some of the city's hidden, meandering waterways with their iconic overhanging willows and rare black poplars was always a treat. While planting a black poplar on Aston's Eyot one day my spade clanked against something hard. I used my hands to dig down a little further and pulled out an intact Victorian pottery hot-water bottle. I wiped off the black dirt to reveal 'Doulton's Improved Foot Warmer' written down both sides. Its RD (registered design) number 200400 dates it to 1893, when the island was used as a rubbish dump. Who knows what other treasures lie beneath the surface there? I was lucky not to smash it and I still have it, some thirty-five years later, a reminder of those Oxford City Council days.

I did the job for two years, eventually gaining the title of Countryside Officer, enjoying life in The Old Courthouse with its coughing ghost on the stairs and hammock slung between contorted apple trees in the old orchard.

I acquired different skills to add to those gained while at Slapton, managing a broad array of nature-rich urban spaces. A green and fascinating city indeed.

However, my heart was still in the windy wilds and salty sea breezes of the West Country. The growing realisation that the increasingly busy Southeast wasn't really for me, and tired of constant traffic, light-polluted skies and some rather testing staff, I found myself on the Quantock Hills.

Chapter Five: 'So where are The Quantocks?'

I was the third Warden for the hills but unlike the first, Colonel Stokes, who often patrolled on horseback, I had a Land Rover, with oak boards bolted to either end of the roof-rack stating 'Quantock Hills Warden' in routed white lettering.

I had seen the job advertised in *The Guardian*'s weekly environment jobs page while on a weekend break down in Slapton and, enticed by the rather unusual name, immediately tried to work out where the Quantock Hills actually were. Completed job applications needed to be sent to the Planning Department at Somerset County Council, so that was a clue. I retrieved the tattered and sun-bleached road map from the back-window shelf of my old Morris Minor; I soon found the Mendips near the long blue ribbon of the M5 and there, further to the south and west running from Taunton up to the

Bristol Channel, was a range of hills with their name proudly written down their spine – Quantock Hills. They seemed intriguing; I don't think I'd ever really noticed them before. I dug out a more detailed map of the area and became rather fascinated by some of the place names: Dead Woman's Ditch, Walford's Gibbet, Slaughterhouse Combe, Wills Neck, Lord's Ball, Great Bear, Grub Bottom and Knacker's Hole. 'Got to be worth a visit anyway,' I said to myself.

This was not quite South Devon, which I had left a couple of years before and was hoping to return to, but it was the Southwest nonetheless – and I'd had enough of Oxford's chaos and increasing urban development. I filled out the job application, slightly daunted by the range of responsibilities listed in the lengthy job description, sent it off to the county council and waited. I soon found out that I had an interview and set off to familiarise myself with the area in preparation.

I drove the old Morris down the motorway towards the west at her optimum cruising speed of 56mph. The wind whistled through the flapping, broken quarter light, the speedo needle oscillated madly, and I fought the vibration in the large, narrow steering wheel. I drove with no radio to keep me company or fifth gear to quiet the ageing engine's whine. On reaching my destination, I explored at a slower pace and was soon captivated by the network of narrow, winding lanes, pretty villages and wonderful vistas of the rolling hills and the sea: a new landscape for me.

I decided to go and have a look at the coast and was immediately mesmerised by the stratified cliffs and gently undulating stony terraces. I sat on the grey, elephant-skin-like rocks at the base of the cliffs looking out towards the islands of Flat Holm and Steep Holm in the Bristol Channel and overheard some holidaymakers discussing what a difficult job it must have been for the council to have laid down such a wonderful pavement for people to walk on! I had to smile.

I headed inland towards Taunton, crossing over the hilltops and having to physically hold the gearstick in second gear to stop it jumping out on the steep 25% descent into the village of Crowcombe. The car and I survived the journey, and, with brake pads still stinking and nerves rather frayed, we pulled into an old schoolmate's shared house where I was staying overnight. I remember having a few too many 'calming' Guinnesses that evening with him and his teacher colleagues and somehow managed to maintain a clear head for my rather formal interview in a very hot and stuffy office in County Hall the next day. A nail-biting week later I had a phone call offering me the job... I said I would take it.

The Quantock Hills lie in an undulating north-westerly line from just above Taunton in the Vale of Taunton Deane to the Bristol Channel coast at Kilve. They are steep on the West Somerset, 'sunset side' of the hills, tapering gently into Sedgemoor in the east: like an aeroplane wing in profile. The hills are about 13 miles long by 3 miles wide and rise to almost 400 metres above sea level, forming some of England's finest countryside. So fine, in fact, that in 1956 they were designated England's first Area of Outstanding Natural Beauty.

Roughly speaking, the southern half of the hills is rolling West Country farmland, narrow lanes and quaint villages; the northern half is wilder, made up of forest, wooded valleys, heathland plateau and coastal limestone cliffs, an incredibly varied mosaic of countryside for a relatively small, protected landscape. From the A358 along their western boundary and from the A39 on their eastern flanks, they appear as an undulating ridge, keeping their interior, the 'heart of the hills' – the heathlands and ancient wooded combes– a well-kept secret from most passers-by.

The ancient oak woodlands in the deep-cut valleys are designated in a block as a Special Area of Conservation. This is a high-level European protection and will hopefully protect these magical woodlands long into the future. Here you find western sessile oaks covered in epiphytes of mosses, lichens and ferns with a carpeted understorey of bright green bilberry and yellow-flowered cow wheat.

These beautiful woods are an important habitat for summer migrants to our western oakwoods such as redstart, wood warbler and pied flycatcher. In addition, there is a wide range of more widespread woodland species including sparrowhawk, tawny owl and all three of our woodpeckers. Other woodland birds include marsh tit and willow tit, nuthatch and treecreeper, thrushes, warblers and finches. Wagtails can be seen flitting up and down the streams and dippers can still be found in small numbers. Along the woodland edges are tree pipit, stonechat and whinchat, yellowhammer and warblers, including grasshopper warbler and whitethroat.

The heathland plateau is also protected (a huge Site of Special Scientific Interest) and has some of the best maritime heath in the country with its associated floral community of ling, bell and bog heather, dwarf western gorse and grasses such as bristle-leaved bent and wavy hair grass. Cowberry (an arctic plant similar to bilberry) is found up on these airy summits, its most southerly known location in the UK, along with heath orchid and sundew in the marshy heads of the combes. In the more open country are skylark and meadow pipit. Buzzards and ravens are easily seen (and heard with their distinctive mewing and cronking). Wheatear is a common migrant and ring ouzels are scarce but regularly seen as they pass through. Hen harrier and merlin are present in very small numbers in winter and the occasional red kite wanders over from their stronghold in central Wales. Kestrels, short-eared owls, Dartford warblers, nightjars, cuckoos and hobbies are just a few of the wonderful birds which can be seen here – and on one freezing winter's day I watched a poor little snow bunting being buffeted around in a blizzard.

The conifer plantations of Great Wood have fewer bird species, but lesser redpoll and siskin are common winter visitors with small numbers of both species breeding here. Crossbills also winter and occasionally nest. A few pairs of nightjars still breed in the recently cut clear-fell areas of the plantations and on some of the open areas of heath.

The Quantocks are rich in prehistoric history with well over fifty Scheduled Ancient Monuments including Bronze Age burial mounds and Iron Age hillforts. It is thought that Quantock derives from an old Celtic word for 'ridge' and that it was the main dividing line between the western tribes, the Dumnonii and the Durotriges.

Moving down to this area was exciting but also testing for our third year of marriage as Jill had only recently accepted her first teaching job in Totnes, 70 miles to the south, and had to fulfil her first year's contract. So, in two separate Morris Minors (the Yukon Grey 1960 saloon and Almond Green 1965 Traveller) loaded to the gunnels with possessions (including cat and cheese plant) and now living in two separate shared houses, the Quantock adventure began. I shared a cottage at Fyne Court in Broomfield (the highest settlement in the hills), and Jilly shared a flat above the chip shop at the top of Totnes High Street. The cottage I was sharing had originally been offered to us as accommodation with the job, but Fyne Court had been broken into and burgled between my interview and starting the job, so the Wildlife Trust had put in a temporary house sitter who refused to leave! This was pretty bad news, but we were now committed to our new venture.

My first day as 'The Warden' involved having my photograph taken outside County Hall for the local newspaper and my Local Authority ID card. I was then driven up into the hills by my new boss Ken Brown and his colleague Alan Watson. Ken was the Countryside Officer for the county council and Alan (a planner) was finalising a new management plan for the hills, and they wanted to properly introduce me to my new 'patch'. We headed out from Taunton in Ken's blue Ford Orion deep in conversation about my new role, and as we travelled along the A358 towards Minehead I began to notice the undulating hills to my right. We seemed to pass alongside them for miles and the scale of the job started to sink in: this was certainly no city country park. I felt slightly nervous now as I began to realise the scope of what my responsibilities were likely to be. I tried to give off a confident and capable air to these two very experienced and knowledgeable council officers.

Ken and Alan were describing the various landmarks along the way and the different landowners and user groups that I would need to actively engage with: important and influential large estate owners, the commoners (hill graziers), the MoD, off-roaders, deer poachers and the hunt. The kind of people I'd never actively 'engaged' with before. This was going to be interesting. Was I in for a baptism of fire?

We pulled off the main road and through the picturesque village of Crowcombe with its thatched, red stone cottages and wound our way up its steep, shady combe and out onto the sunny hilltops. The landscape opened up around us with swathes of bracken, patches of heather and windswept, contorted hawthorn trees. It felt wild and wind-blown, very different from the cosy, pastoral farmland below.

After about half a mile of heading east along a narrow, unfenced road and carefully avoiding potholes and occasional sheep lying on the tarmac, we pulled into a rough, stony car park and climbed out of the confines of the car. It was wonderful to be out in the cool, breezy air and big skies; the expansive views were breath-taking. To the north I could see rolling heather-clad hills falling away to the shining Severn Sea mottled with dark cloud shadows racing across the water, and in the distance the unmistakable profile of Pen-y-Fan in the Brecon Beacons.

Between the hills were deep, wooded valleys that looked forgotten by time. In the hazy east the flat lands of the Somerset Levels and Moors ended where the Mendip Hills began, and to the south the deep-green forest dominated the near landscape with the hills' highest point, Wills Neck, sitting proudly above the trees. To the west the Quantocks seemed to merge effortlessly with the Brendon Hills and Exmoor uplands, with Somerset's highest point Dunkery Beacon crouched on the horizon. The only sound was the wind in the old hawthorns and invisible skylarks singing somewhere in the blue, high above.

'Right,' said Ken, 'this is your patch. Over the next few months get to know the hills and the people who live here and use them.'

I remember that moment very well even today, more than thirty years later. I felt a mixed sense of unbelievable freedom and the weight of responsibility and trust that Ken had put in me to do the job. I couldn't mess it up. Where was I to start? What does the only warden out here do on a daily basis? How was I going to get around this seemingly vast and lumpy landscape?

I had desperately wanted to be working in the wider countryside, in landscape-scale conservation... now I was there!

'You'll need a Land Rover,' said Ken. 'We'll get one ordered.' This was music to my ears. I had spent the last two years bumping around Oxford in my old faithful white City Council one. 'Not a bad first day at work,' I thought to myself as we headed back towards Taunton and the modern world. However, the honeymoon period didn't last long.

I had to wait a few weeks for the purchase of the Land Rover to go through the snail's pace of local authority procurement processes. In the meantime, I was given a bright yellow Vauxhall Astra van with Somerset County Council (and its Wyvern dragon logo) proudly emblazoned in red on its sides. It was a rather unsubtle mode of transport to be arriving in at remote valley farmyards or busy weekend hilltop car parks, but this was only my first few weeks, and I was sure that the locals would be welcoming their new 'hills protector' with open arms and imagined, traditional West Country smiles.

But this was deepest, darkest Somerset and the locals were hardy hill farmers and stag hunters and most of them, it appeared, seemed to vehemently loathe the council.

What had I done? Where had I come to? I had only ever really passed through Somerset on the M5 on the way to Devon or Cornwall before now and been to Glastonbury Festival once (although I couldn't remember too much about it!). How was I going to survive this?

Chapter Six: Early days

To guide the way the hills were managed, a brand new and comprehensive management plan had just been published by the time I took up post in the Quantocks, and one of my first jobs was to deliver it to landowners, farmers and user groups throughout the area. This gave me the perfect opportunity to introduce myself. By now I had a uniform and a badge to compliment the Land Rover, and at last felt that I could officially represent the AONB as its sole officer on the ground. Its 'Lone Ranger'.

The management plan was a new venture for the council who, unlike some other local authority planning departments at the time, took its role in countryside and heritage protection very seriously. This was probably down to the enthusiastic support from influential county councillors such as Lady Gass and conscientious, determined officers like Ken Brown and

Alan Watson in Countryside and Bob Croft in Heritage. Somerset had two AONBs and both now had full-time wardens: Tom Elkin on the Mendips (soon to be replaced by Les Davies) and me on the Quantocks. Les was awarded an MBE for his services to the environment... he really is 'Mr Mendip' as far as many people are concerned. Lone wardens on our hilltop islands separated by the sea of the misty Somerset Levels and Moors. Alan's management plan was soon to receive praise from the Landscape Planning Institute, a first for this kind of plan, and he was invited to receive his award from Prince Charles.

With bundles of the newly published plan piled up on the passenger seat I set about distributing them. This meant trying to phone farmers or landowners to arrange a visit, but more often than not usually ended up with me arriving unannounced in the farmyard and knocking on the farmhouse kitchen door to a mixed reception. Was I going to be 'ripped apart' physically by a protective farm dog or verbally from some irate farmer whose precious time I would undoubtedly be wasting?

'I think we know how to look after our own hills thank you very much, and we don't need any new management plan from the county council to tell us how to do it!' was a fairly common response. 'OK... just be polite and patient,' I thought to myself.

After initial mistrust and/or scepticism, I would often be invited into the farmhouse kitchen and offered a mug of tea for a good chat or moan about the lack of Government funding for farmers, too many visitors, too many dogs, too many new-fangled mountain bikes... and the county council in general. I think that this was an opportunity for them to get a few frustrations out. I would pretty quickly be asked what I thought about stag hunting. This was difficult, because to be honest I loathed the very idea of chasing any animal to exhaustion and then killing it for fun. It seemed immoral, cruel and wholly unjustified, especially killing a creature as majestic as a wild red deer stag. A more iconic representation of British wildness I could hardly imagine. If they were as busy as they always claimed to be, how did they have time to spend two days a week tearing around the hills chasing deer? They were obviously wanting to establish whether this new 'greenhorn' of a warden was an 'anti' or not. I generally responded that it wasn't for me, that I was genuinely a country boy at heart, I had other recreational interests and that part of my job was to protect the hills from unnecessary damage or disturbance (of which the hunt followers in their 4x4s, quad bikes and motorbikes were undeniably a major contributor). Even this response was usually received defensively. I hadn't realised just how sensitive and all-encompassing an issue this whole hunting debate was – I was sailing into choppy waters.

My visits also took me to large and well-established family estates. Driving down long tree-lined avenues to arrive at a huge country pile felt very much like going to see the 'Lord of the Manor'. The Quantocks are a feudal place, with large country estates surrounded by tenanted farms. One of the reasons that the hills have survived relatively intact from intensive farming 'improvements' or development is partly due to these unbroken estates and the tracts of common land attached to them. Large areas of heathland, woodland, coast and farmland dominate the northern half of the AONB and contain most of its extensive landscapes and special wildlife. It is these estates that have had layers of landscape and environmental protective legislation placed upon them over the decades whether they liked it or not, so political sensitivity and diplomacy in any discussions with the landowners was paramount.

I was beginning to realise that my role was much more that of a diplomat than just being an 'on the ground' warden patrolling the hills, giving guided walks and picking up litter. It was a far more multi-layered, complex and sensitive place than I had imagined. This job was going to require all the 'people skills' and 'survival skills' that I could muster.

Forming useful allies was going to be vital; perhaps I should start with these influential major landowners and see how I get on? I decided to call on Lady Gass who owned Fairfield Estate. From conversations I had heard in County Hall I knew that she would be supportive; being Chairman of Exmoor National Park Authority should help.

I drove down her long drive through ancient parkland, admiring the veteran trees, and arrived on the gravel at the front of the house to be met by the gardener. He escorted me around to the back where I waited on the cobbles of the old courtyard beside a large, lead water pump.

Lady Gass soon arrived with a couple of small, yapping border terriers and led me down a dark, narrow corridor into a tiny kitchen. It was rather surreal; the house was huge, its panelled dining room with ancestral portraits breath-taking, and yet meetings were held in a minute, magnolia-coloured kitchen tucked away in the old servants' quarters. I guess that's how she liked it – she lived alone and must have rattled around in that big old place. The comforting warmth of the ancient AGA must have been a very dear friend in the cold winter months. Lady Gass was very welcoming, interested in the new management plan and seemed very pleased to have a new, enthusiastic young warden to help keep an eye on her huge estate. This included some of the best habitats and landscape within the AONB, from seashore through wooded valleys up to the heathy summits.

I was to have many meetings with Lady Gass over the following years – she was an extremely supportive and influential landowner. She was often 'bad mouthed' by the hunting fraternity, probably as a result of her stopping them hunting on her land on Saturdays. Lady Gass was from the Acland family, previous owners of Holnicote and Killerton Estates, now in the capable hands of the National Trust.

Holnicote Estate must be one of the jewels in the crown for the Trust, a wonderful and vitally important National Nature Reserve, a mix of heathland, ancient oak woods, rivers, tall-chimneyed sandstone villages and dramatic coast just west of Minehead, overlooked by Somerset's highest hilltop, Dunkery Beacon.

My first visit to see Sir Walter Luttrell (Lord Lieutenant) on the coast at East Quantoxhead Estate did not go quite so well. Again, on arrival I was escorted through the garden by an aged employee and up to the huge stone castellated house to be met by the very tall and elegantly dressed Colonel. 'Good afternoon Mr Russell, nice to meet you at last, do come in,' he said politely in a deep voice. 'What can I get you to drink? Cup of tea, a beer, Madeira, whisky?' He was terribly well-spoken.

'Ooh, a beer would be very nice, thank you very much,' I replied, thinking that this would be a more bonding and relaxed way to initiate a conversation. We sat down to discuss the new management plan and my new job. It was all very formal, and I was trying my best to appear grown-up, reliable and sensible when, all of a sudden, I sent the full glass flying off the side table showering its contents across a very expensive-looking Persian carpet. 'Oh, sorry!' I said. 'Shall I get a cloth?' 'Too late for that now!' he boomed.

Over the years I spoke to Colonel Luttrell on numerous occasions, generally about military use of his estate (of which he was very supportive and in which he took a great interest) or public access issues with his tenant farmers. He was an extremely charming, polite and interesting man. On one visit to his ancient homestead, not long before his death, he invited me in for a more informal chat and poured me a frighteningly large whisky; it seemed he just wanted to talk about the past. He recalled growing up in Dunster Castle as a child and having the first Mercedes sports car in Somerset, with which he set fire to the moors when he drove it across the heathery uplands one hot, dry summer in the 1920s. I really should not have driven back to the office after that visit, but I got away with it! His brother sold Dunster Castle to the National Trust in the 1970s for £1. I attended Sir Walter's funeral in Dunster, a very moving event with Royal Household Cavalry playing their trumpets in the church and a rather grand wake in the huge, ancient tithe barn. It felt like the end of an era that stretched back unbroken to the Norman invasion. William the Conqueror had given the Luttrell family these lands 1000 years before.

OK... the next important landowner on the list was 'The Major' of Crowcombe Estate. He once owned Crowcombe Court, a magnificent Georgian house nestled under the wooded western scarp of the hills amongst ancient parkland oaks. The house was accessed down a long straight drive behind the beautiful village church, but the Major now lived in 'The Bungalow', a modern yellow building close by. I pulled into the driveway and was loudly told, 'He's inside!' I knocked on the door and was called through to his study with a bellowing, 'Come in!' The Major, a large man, was silhouetted behind his desk. It felt a bit like being summoned to see the headmaster. I entered the room; it was one of the strangest moments I can recall. We were in a modern bungalow and yet here I was in a 'Victorian' dark wood-panelled study with the walls covered in hunting trophies of all kinds. I didn't know where to look first as I took in the many sets of antlers, deer heads, fox heads, badger and otter heads all with bared teeth staring down at me between sets of deer feet also attached to the wall on wooden plaques.

I refocused on the Major, moustached and smoking a large cigar… was I in some sort of time warp? Had I just come through some magic wardrobe? I felt I was interrupting his day. I didn't know quite how to start up a normal conversation so began telling him that I had just seen a yellow VW Beetle in the woods of the park beyond the 'Private No Entry' sign, probably not where he would have liked it to be, and did he know about it?

'Oh God, I suppose I'll have to inform MAFF now!' he blurted. I can only assume that he must have thought I was referring to the Colorado beetle, a black and yellow pest of potato crops in the 1970s.

The last time I saw him, many years later, he was sitting astride a huge horse, crop in hand, on the Old Drove Road in the mist and relentless drizzle on a cold hunting day. He was a larger-than-life character, the first Chairman of the Exmoor National Park Committee. Quantock Committees held in County Hall started at 2.15pm at his bidding instead of 2pm to allow for 'Quantock Time' (whatever that was). I understand that at his funeral his coffin was laid out on gorse cut from the hills.

My next visit was to see Geoffrey King. Mr King owned Bagborough Estate (which includes Wills Neck, the highest point of the hills), part of which, Triscombe Quarry, he had sold to Tarmac. This was an active quarry when I started work on the hills, a huge scar which glowed pink in the sunset. It is now developing as a wonderful nature reserve with a lake, young trees and nesting peregrine falcons on its weathering cliffs. His estate also included tenanted sandstone cottages in and around West Bagborough. Visiting Mr King's office for my once and only time was like stepping back to Scrooge's office in Dickensian London. A single-bar electric fire barely heated the tiny, cramped room. Mr King was friendly and chatty and delighted in reaching up to old, rolled-up estate maps on dusty shelves to show me the detail and extent of his estate. He advised me to liaise with his Estate Manager, Mr Hawthorn, in any matters relating to the estate from then on. I don't think I ever saw Mr King ever again in all of my twenty-five years, although we occasionally exchanged letters. It was all very quaint and old fashioned, a snapshot from a bygone era.

The Warmingtons had Cothelstone Estate, a stunningly beautiful area just east of Bishops Lydeard. Cothelstone Manor and church are tucked under the steep backdrop of the hills, a more quintessential English landscape would be hard to find. During his notorious Assizes of 1642–51, Judge Jeffreys had two of the estate staff hung from the arched gateway. Cothelstone Hill had been sold to the county council in the 1970s and was now one of my most important sites to manage. We rented one of the estate's red sandstone cottages in Lower Terhill for over fifteen years and came to know the family well.

They used to kindly lay on a Christmas party in the little wooden village hall for all of the children living on the estate, my daughters included. Hugh Warmington would dress up as Santa and hand out presents from a large hessian sack.

Then there were party games such as 'Oranges and Lemons', followed by orange squash, ice-cream and jelly. A long-standing estate tradition.

Jane Warmington had been the area's Farming and Wildlife Advisory Group officer before marrying Hugh. We all shared similar views on land management and conservation and had many useful conversations (and cups of tea) sitting at the pine kitchen table in front of the huge cream AGA. It often felt like being in a scene from *The Archers*. In fact, the agricultural script writer lived in the same village as one of my work colleagues, so I can guess that some of the show's storyline ideas may have possibly come from him. Hugh's level-headed Chairmanship of the Deer Management and Conservation Group helped to steer and calm some often overheated, entrenched and opinionated discussions on the subject.

My first meeting with the MoD at Norton Manor Camp is quite memorable too. Forty Commando Royal Marines who were based there were recently back from manoeuvres in Belize and wanted to discuss their new training regime on the hills. They asked if I could go over and look at some maps with them. Having never been on a military base in my life before, this sounded quite intriguing. On arrival, I was politely greeted by the Camp's Adjutant and swiftly escorted to meet the new Commanding Officer.

We started to pour over maps of the area, and I did my best to gently remind him that the hills were not in fact an officially designated military training area. They had specific protection and that there were genuine sensitivities and laws about where vehicles could be driven and guns could be carried, and that different landowners had different rules.

'Why don't we just do this from the air?' the Commanding Officer suggested, obviously getting a little impatient. I was led out to a Lynx helicopter in a state of surprise and disbelief, and without further ado we rapidly launched into the skies. This was my first flight in a helicopter, and it didn't go too well. I was seated in the back, squeezed next to the CO, the pilot directly in front. Unfortunately for me the pilot hadn't long come back from the Falklands and was throwing the machine around as if he was trying to evade enemy fire!

The rotor blades strobing above me through the glass roof were starting to make me feel dizzy; I could feel my face drain, my skin and hands become clammy… I was going to be sick. 'Do you have any sick bags?' I asked embarrassingly via the helmet microphone. 'They're in the door pocket.' I couldn't find any. The officer rolled his eyes in frustration and fumbled around in his briefcase for envelopes and eventually found one. I made use of it. He then instructed the pilot to land for a few minutes in a forest clearing for me to sort myself out. I wasn't too bad after that; the pilot flew more gently (enemy fire had obviously ceased) and we could properly work out their required rendezvous points on the ground below.

To my surprise we then headed north to the Bristol Channel and landed at Colonel Luttrell's house for a quick chat and a cup of tea (in his capacity as Lord Lieutenant I imagine) – all quite surreal. Despite the queasy flight, seeing the folded and forested hills and grey expanse of sea from the air for the first time was magical.

I was lucky enough to have a few more helicopter flights over the years, and these were due to aerial bracken spraying. We had tried doing this work with tractor-mounted booms, but the ground was too steep and bumpy over much of the area, so helicopters were used. The pilots were keen to have the exact area properly identified prior to spraying so asked if I could go up with them on an initial flight. These small, lightweight helicopters, adapted for crop spraying, were a different breed altogether from the military Lynx. They resembled the Perspex-domed helicopter I could remember from the *Skippy the Bush Kangaroo* TV series. Two tiny seats inside a bubble, no doors, and a 'Meccano' style construction. The pilot treated me to an almost heart-stopping low-level flight, dropping down into the wooded valleys, flying just above the treetops and bush-hopping back across the heathland at about 70mph just a few feet from the ground... exhilarating to say the least.

One pilot asked if I would mind if he let his machine free-fall to test his gearing system. We rose vertically into the sky above Dead Woman's Ditch (the highest I had been so far – I could see for miles). 'Do I have much of a choice?' I asked. 'Not really,' he replied with a wry smile. I was putting all my trust and faith into this pilot and his machine, so I held on tight to the tiny seat, barely able to calm my nerves.

Basically he put it into neutral and let it drop towards the earth, a very strange feeling. The gearing worked and he was able to control its free-fall. It was quite a ride, a one-off experience, although not one I would necessarily want to repeat.

For much of the time during my first year as warden I was by myself: just me, my Land Rover and the hills. Exploring this new world, uncharted territory for me, at my own pace and meeting lots of new and interesting people was a privilege and a learning experience that I won't forget. This was my 'office', my 'factory floor' and it was all new to me. Although only 40 square miles in size, the Quantocks are an intimate mosaic of lanes, villages, woods, heathlands, forest and farmland. They seem much bigger than they actually are due to the topography of deep valleys and sweeping vistas. I was beginning to put their layout into some sort of order in my head, trying to visualise the country from the contours and colours on the map. Rather blurred memories and slightly traumatic flashbacks from the helicopter flight helped a bit.

One area that stood out from the map, made up of tightly swirling rust-coloured contour lines and a large green splodge, was Great Wood (or Quantock Forest) which formed a huge dark saddle, a central wooded belt separating the southern and northern commons. It merged with the ancient oak woods near Dead Woman's Ditch which ran unbroken to Holford. Great Wood used to belong to Lord Taunton as part of the huge Quantock Estate. It was felled during the First World War and sold to the county council who then leased it to the newly formed Forestry Commission. Similar actions took place all over rural England at the time, the breaking up of large family estates and the planting of dark, straight-lined blocks of alien conifers to replace much that had been lost in the war effort.

As the forest was owned by the county council and only leased to the Forestry Commission it formed part of my official patrol area and it was an enticing place to explore, but getting disorientated there was easy. Huge, impressive Douglas fir trees (some of the tallest in the country) closed the view and dense conifer plantations formed impenetrable walls. However, remnants of the original deciduous oak forest allowed light into forgotten corners, allowing carpets of bilberry and grasses to flourish. It was here that you could find deer sheltering in this quiet green sanctuary, away from people and in the lee of the prevailing southwesterlies.

A network of gravel tracks ran along most of the valley bottoms and ridges allowing access to much of the forest; I began to venture into here more often and to call in at the Forestry Office. This was a small wooden building that resembled a US Ranger Outpost and was a welcome place for grabbing a coffee and sharing local news. There was always something to talk about, whether it was reports on suspected poachers, the activities of the hunt, where decent deer stags were currently 'holding up' or any good bird sightings such as goshawk, nightjar or crossbills.

The foresters were pretty 'old school'; this was still the 1980s and forest management seemed more focused on timber production than wildlife conservation or recreational use. It all seemed very 'Civil Service', a blast from the 1950s, with dull, dark-brown desks, in-trays and out-trays and even duller beige filing cabinets – it made County Hall seem very up to date. Nick Best was the Forest Officer at this time and was a particularly pleasant, funny, softly spoken man who bought his sandwiches to work in a wicker pannier basket. Eric Smith was a ranger who would occasionally visit from his main patch in the quiet depths of the Brendon Hills. He knew a lot about deer and poaching and was always fascinating to listen to in between his constant cigarette puffs.

Nick was a man of the office, Eric a man of the forest with a battle-scarred, mud-splattered Land Rover and Government Issue rifle. I warmed to him quickly; he seemed to be from a hidden world that normal mortals never saw, like Strider in *The Lord of The Rings*, a lone ranger from the wastelands. He probably viewed me as some greenhorn college boy from Oxford who knew nothing about West Somerset ways or real ranger work. He was probably right; I had a lot to learn.

Getting out and about with my bosses Ken and Alan was always welcome. They would occasionally manage to get out of Taunton – I think coming to support or 'check-up' on me was a great excuse to escape the constant meetings, letter writing and local politics, which I could totally understand!

In those days, letters and reports were all written by hand for secretaries to type up, copy in triplicate and bring back for signing. Alan always wrote with a fountain pen in his distinctive brown ink and impeccable handwriting; I scribbled with cheap Bic biros squirrelled from secret stationery cupboard raids when visiting County Hall.

One of his interests was photography, and whenever he came out onto the hills he had his faithful SLR slung over his shoulder. Fuji slide film was what we used in those days, and we amassed many images over the years which were mainly used in slide shows and committee reports using noisy fan-cooled projectors with annoying, vibrating Kodak slide carousels. Loading slides into these, I remember, was always 'upside down and back to front'. It all seems so old-fashioned and laboured now in this slick, quick PowerPoint age.

One day, Alan suggested that now it was autumn we ought to get out on foot and witness the deer rut, a dramatic annual event when the red deer stags defend their harem of hinds and fend off any male competitors. Alan wanted some nice misty autumn shots of the hills, and if there were any deer around that would be a bonus.

It was a corker of a day as we walked out onto the heath from Lydeard Hill car park: honey-brown bracken, champagne air, clear blue skies and buzzards mewing overhead. The views into the vale were obscured by a brilliant, white mist below us and bright sunshine above. Perhaps the Quantocks at their best. Those of you who have been up on the hills on one of these 'inversion days' will appreciate how wonderful it can be... you feel on top of the world; the Quantocks literally become their own sunny island surrounded by a brilliant and bubbling sea of white cloud. On occasion, only the distant tower on top of Glastonbury Tor and the Wellington Monument atop the Blackdown Hills could be seen protruding above the cloud.

Some of the beech trees were half in mist as we approached Bagborough Woods making the place 'otherworldly' and very photogenic, so Alan's camera was constantly clicking beside me. These beech woods, with their old and misshapen trees, are particularly evocative in the mist or fog and have a surreal depth and silence to them; you can quickly leave the real world behind you. We eventually emerged from the woods out onto the heath and into the sunshine and the wider world.

We sat down in the autumn sun on the steep hillside and could just about hear the traffic, invisible through the dense mist below us on the A358. In the distance the Wellington Monument was just poking through the top of the cloud bank; a good time for a coffee, we thought. Suddenly, somewhere below us in the murk, I heard a mighty roar that made the hair on the back of my neck rise. It was a deep, guttural, ancient sound... and out of nowhere a huge stag appeared from the trees below us.

Oh, my goodness, – I had never heard or been so close to a wild stag before! I was transfixed to the spot in both fear and fascination. We were completely in the open, sitting down, nowhere to go. What was it going to do? Had it seen us yet? Where were his hinds? Were we between them and him? Which way was the wind blowing? Can he smell us? Was he angry? Stay still or run? Lots of questions rushed through my unprepared and inexperienced brain.

This was a rare stag, a twelve pointer, a Royal. I'm sure that they're even rarer now. It was huge and looked majestic, powerful and dangerous. 'What do we do?' I whispered (or squeaked) to Alan, trying to be as quiet as I possibly could. I can't remember the exact detail, but we quietly monitored its movements as it paused for a few moments. Had it heard me? Had he smelt us? Something caught its attention, and it started to march through the heather and bilberry towards us in a very deliberate and determined manner. I couldn't bear staying put any longer so moved stealthily towards an isolated rhododendron bush and crouched directly behind it, trying to make myself invisible. The stag proudly strode right past me, up over the earth bank and out of sight. I could hear its great bulk crashing through the vegetation and its heavy breathing. It was close, it was in the open and it had been my first encounter with a wild stag during the rut – I won't ever forget it. Alan got some great shots, and I really needed that coffee! What a morning – this job certainly had its memorable moments.

Alan became a great friend over the next twenty-five years, a kindred spirit in all that was wild and free. We gained a deep love and respect for this small, little-known range of English hills, birds of prey and the Native American 'Earth Spirit' connection with the natural world which we were both interested in. Alan later became a planner for the National Trust but sadly died of cancer not long after his fiftieth birthday. I placed a buzzard feather on his wicker coffin as it was being lowered; I like to think that his spirit is soaring somewhere beautiful still. He introduced me to Fairport Convention, we saw some gigs, and I think of him whenever I hear 'Meet on The Ledge'. He is greatly missed by all who knew him.

Towards the end of my first year I was approached by Chris Edwards, a postgraduate student studying environmental management and in need of a relevant work placement. We got on well and it would be good for me to have some company and an extra pair of hands. I talked the proposition through with Ken and it was agreed. I soon discovered that Chris was a great orator, a wordsmith, and that he liked writing reports; he could type and had a computer (well, sort of). We jointly conceived our quarterly reports and necessary letter writing on Chris's Amstrad, sitting in the old bathroom of his flat at Triscombe House, the computer perched on a wooden board over the old cast iron bath! This was our office for a brief period. It was cold and slightly weird sharing a 'bathroom office' together, but there were great views through the window of the steeply sloping flanks of Bagborough Hill where we would occasionally see the White Hind (a particularly rare red deer, not an albino) which had become somewhat of a local celebrity. This was always a very welcome distraction from report writing.

Chris also had his own car, a little boxy Fiat Panda 4x4 (you rarely see them any more), and when he pulled up next to my Defender, it looked like it had just had a baby. I was quite impressed by it really – it looked pretty cool.

A year later Chris applied for the new post of Assistant Warden, and got the job. We were now a team... a Warden Service! We needed to get him an official work vehicle, but budgets were a bit tighter, and we were also having to pay him! We acquired a second-hand, early 1980s beige Subaru pickup from Hugh Warmington for a few hundred quid, but I knew that they were great little workhorses. Les and Tina, the Mendip Wardens, swore by them and had them for years.

Chris's first few weeks as a warden were rather similar to mine. The first time he filled up his newly signed pick-up at Flaxpool Garage a local farmer (who shall remain nameless) greeted him with: 'Looks like someone else is 'ere to waste our time an' money and tell us what we can't do!' Welcome aboard, Chris. One of his first excursions onto the hills was quite memorable. The Subaru had less ground clearance than my Land Rover and while he was following me through a sandy area near Bicknoller Post his vehicle sank up to its belly in dry sand, four wheels spinning madly and spraying sand everywhere. I had to tow him out.

A few months after this event we were helping to film a regional documentary programme called *Not the M5*, about the interesting places in the West Country to be discovered on or near the A38. Nether Stowey was chosen as a destination of interest for its historical associations with the Romantic Poets, Coleridge and Wordsworth, and of course the beauty of the Quantock Hills themselves. We wanted to use this opportunity to raise the issue of the fragility of the hills to erosion and vehicle damage to the wider public, so we went up to the hilltops to do the interview.

I was doing my piece to camera and Chris was going to trundle up in his truck driving very carefully to join us and do his bit. The interviewer and I waited and waited. No sign of Chris but we could hear the frantic revving of a highly squealing engine from over the ridge of the grassy knoll. We decided to investigate and discovered Chris unsuccessfully trying to clear the summit and, in the process, turning the hillside into what resembled a ploughed field. So much for protecting the hills from vehicle damage! Chris was wearing a huge pair of rabbit skin gloves (recently inherited from his uncle, a former Dartmoor prison warder) and it looked as if two possessed rabbits had taken control of his steering wheel! This seemed a much more comical version of the darker Dartmoor legend, further down the A38, where a pair of Hairy Hands are alleged to take hold of the victim's steering wheel and direct their vehicle off the road to their doom!

Unsurprisingly the Subaru didn't last too long! Through the Fire Brigade we were offered the old Burnham on Sea cliff rescue long-wheelbase Land Rover, complete with roof-top ladder. This vehicle truly was a beast; it guzzled petrol, had a pathetic turning circle, no power steering and ended up in the Fire Service Museum a year later.

Most warden jobs involve digging holes; I dread to think of the number of holes I have had to dig over the last thirty years or so. Planting trees and the installation of most infrastructure requires a hole, eg fingerposts, waymarker posts, gate posts, straining posts, fenceposts, fire beater hanging posts, boardwalk supports, interpretation panel legs, picnic table legs and bollards.

Chris and I needed to dig in some wooden bollards to prevent the unauthorised and damaging spread of motor vehicles parking at a site called Sandy Beds. We had quite a number to do so thought that it would make sense to hire a petrol-powered auger. We chose a two-man high-powered version with an eight-inch wide drill. What could possibly go wrong?

It was extremely heavy and had triangular handlebars on either side. We dragged it off the trailer and stood the thing up; it looked a ferocious beast. 'OK, let's give it go...' I gingerly suggested.

The start cord was pulled, and the machine revved into life. We positioned it over the first spot, trying to keep it upright and revved it even higher, and the auger started to bury itself slowly into the stony ground. 'Give it some more umph!' shouted Chris through the mad clatter and exhaust fumes. I did. The machine became manic, spraying earth and stones in every direction. Suddenly, without warning, the auger hit bedrock and stopped dead, the handlebars spun instead. Chris and I were instantly launched into the air in opposite directions, Chris ended up in a gorse bush and I ended up in some brambles! If mobile phones had been around at the time someone could have earned themselves a rather easy £250 on *You've Been Framed*!

Our landings had been thankfully somewhat cushioned, but by the worst cushions available. We were rather shaken, but glad that our backs hadn't been irreparably twisted. We dug the bollards in after that. Augers are probably great for digging holes on the beach. Why the site was called Sandy Beds we'll never know – it certainly had no sand.

Chris slipped his disc (I hope that there was no connection to the auger incident) and was laid up in bed for months. We kept him busy colouring in land ownership maps, and he compiled a comprehensive and very useful Voluntary Wardens' Handbook. I needed to park my Land Rover in a nearby Taunton backstreet when visiting him a couple of times each week. Word soon got around, and I was suspected of having an affair... aah, the good old bush telegraph!

Chris and I were often called upon to give talks to local interest groups. We usually shared this aspect of the job as these were mostly evening talks that followed a Parish Council, Wildlife Trust, Rotary or other local group's AGM. We would take along a screen, projector and carousel of around sixty slides (roughly a slide a minute) and give an illustrated talk about the AONB, its wonderful landscapes, its special wildlife and our role as wardens. We usually enjoyed these talks; they were a great way to get our message across to members of the local population (sometimes quite influential) as a 'captive audience'.

On occasion, though, as part of the evening's proceedings, we would be asked to judge a competition. This is where it could get a bit tricky, although it filled one with a strange sense of power! I can particularly recall being asked to judge a floral competition for the Carhampton Gardening Society. It was obvious that some of the more 'well to do' members of the society had been able to put together some incredibly 'over the top' arrangements.

One very elderly little lady (bent double with age) had meekly placed a few snowdrops in an old glass inkpot... the subtlety of this minimal, botanic submission delighted me. It was rather poignant in its simplicity compared to the other displays. I gave it first prize, much to the disdain and obvious irritation of the chairperson and higher echelons of the assembled group. The next time I was invited back to give a talk, some years later when the 'political dust' had settled, I was asked to judge the potatoes!

Chapter Seven: Fighting Fire with Fire

I can remember Chris's first official day at work pretty well: it was hot and dry and looked like it was going to be a stunning, clear evening for views. We thought we'd finish the day on the top of Lydeard Hill, to 'breathe in' his new patch (we had decided to split our patrol areas to the north and south areas of the AONB, and Chris had the south as he lived in Taunton). We left the truck in the car park and started to walk out onto the hills where we quickly noticed a plume of smoke rising into the sky above Wills Neck. Oh no!

A summer fire, something I'd dreaded. Not being entirely sure how to handle this we ran back to the car park to grab some fire beaters leaning next to the gate and headed out quickly towards the fire. Pretty quickly a red, canvas-topped Fire Brigade Land Rover bounced its dusty way across Aisholt Common and joined us. We beat the fire out with the wooden-handled fire beaters, a number of them snapping with old age and the rubber flaps melted and limp.

We were lucky; the ling heather was short, and we managed to get the fire under control. Must get some decent fire beaters, I noted.

Summer fires are devastating as they burn the roots of the heather and usually kill it. The hill graziers hadn't done any controlled burning for thirteen years or so due to insurance uncertainties, and the heathlands were becoming derelict with dense scrub and gorse and prone to large summer fires. It was clear that we needed to get a properly planned and controlled burning regime back in place.

For thousands of years the Quantock heathlands were managed using fire, allowing fresh vegetation to flourish for the grazing animals of the Neolithic and Bronze Age settlers. Heathland is a manmade habitat at low altitudes and has replaced the woodland that was once there. Because it is now a valuable and threatened wildlife habitat, part of our job was to conserve it (ironically, it seemed to most people) by setting it on fire.

With new yellow-handled fiberglass fire beaters (sourced from Southern California) we established a network of beater stations throughout the hilltops, accessible at the main access points to the commons. We also had a few strapped to the top of the Land Rover to be at hand whenever needed and for swaling (our ecological burns) during the early spring months. A fifteen-year, rotational cycle of controlled burns was mapped with help from English Nature, and we were ready to get started.

The first few swaling episodes were fairly memorable. We'd never done it before, and it was pretty stressful setting fire to acres of heathland and scrub and not really knowing where it would stop. In those early days we tied diesel-soaked rags to bent clothes hangers and used them as torches, lighting the heather and gorse as we walked along the planned edge. We had no estate team (unlike our nearby Exmoor National Park colleagues) and so were helped by volunteers; we assumed that eroded tracks and short wet grass would act as fire breaks, they usually did.

The first group of volunteers turned up in their Ford Transit minibus and we advised them to park it well out of the way on a nearby track. Pretty soon the fire was raging uphill, and the van was completely obscured by the grey smoke. 'Shit, where's the van?' was the question on everyone's mind. Chris grabbed the keys from one of the volunteers and raced off in the Subaru to find it and move it out of the smoke and menacing, advancing flames. For a moment or two there was an eerie silence as he disappeared into the dense smoke, then the awful, high-pitched sound of a squealing engine pierced the thick air. Not again! I ran over to where the sound was coming from. Chris had somehow managed to drive on top of the ancient field boundary bank that marked the edge of our burn and had been invisible in the smoke, all four wheels were spinning in the air, the vehicle rocking on its belly, going nowhere fast.

I sprinted to my Land Rover, trying not to display my panic to the open-mouthed volunteers. Setting fire to their van on our first swale would not be good. I quickly grabbed a chain from the back, hooked it to the front of the Subaru and pulled Chris off the bank, much to his relief. All vehicles were soon out of the way, embarrassment averted, and nerves slightly calmed with coffee and custard creams (essential volunteer fuel).

Lessons learned: don't burn uphill unless you have a fire break you can totally trust, park any vehicles upwind of the fire, leave the keys in the vehicle, get some two-way radios, make sure the fire breaks are wide enough and carry out a controlled back burn first.

Doing a controlled back burn isn't always easy; you're trying to burn a section of heath a few metres wide for the approaching main fire wall to reach and then stop. Nothing stops a fire better than an already burnt patch with no fuel in it. The trouble is you can't let it get going too much otherwise you can lose control of it and then you're in trouble. So doing a back burn from a decent fire break is essential.

We often used this method when fighting wildfires, much to the curiosity of the Fire Brigade who refused to attempt this as legally they're not allowed to actually start fires, only put them out (or so they told us anyway). So, we'd often be downwind of a wildfire starting a new one to create a break while they'd be at the other end putting it out. However, we developed an excellent working relationship with them and would sometimes be the first to report a fire and help in its containment.

On one such occasion (as mentioned earlier), I didn't quite make the 'helping with the containment' bit as I managed to 'contain' my Land Rover in a rather deep slurry pit! I had seen smoke drifting above the dense silver birch and deep gorse of Great Bear (the site of the Quantock's worst summer fire some twenty years before) and knew that this wasn't good; the area was difficult to get to and virtually impenetrable. My job was to race out across the fields below the fire, report back on its progress and seek out any suitable vehicle access for bringing in firefighters and water to tackle the blaze.

The paddock grasses were yellow; it had been dry for a while, and the grass growing on top of the slurry pit had also burnt yellow so I didn't know it was there. To my surprise my vehicle came to a very unexpected stop, I lurched forward, and it slowly began to sink. It rolled onto the driver's side and sunk further into the pit. It got dark. I guess that I was panicking a little by now, but it all seemed to happen in slow motion. I looked for the light and clambered out of the passenger door window and shakily stood on solid ground, my Land Rover like a culled beast beside me. I rather embarrassingly contacted the Fire Brigade to explain my predicament. Jeez, only I could do this. I was going to be the laughingstock of the hills!

Getting the thing out was going to be no easy task. Had I wrecked it? Think quickly – who did I know with a decent tractor? I phoned Bill Fewings at Quantock Farm. He chuckled and agreed to come and pull me out; he couldn't wait to see the warden in a pickle. He turned up some time later, put a chain around the front of the Land Rover and revved the tractor, but it wasn't having it; the sunken vehicle stayed where it was. He shrugged his shoulders, disappeared with the tractor and returned with an even bigger chain and bigger tractor, and this time it worked. Inch by inch the semi-buried slurry beast was pulled free. Somehow or other the faithful old Land Rover blurted back into life; it was definitely the tool for the job. It was all a little embarrassing and rather unnerving at the time, but I sometimes recall the event, and it's a great dinner party anecdote.

Chris and I unfortunately needed Bill and his big tractor again six months later. Chris had decided to attempt the steep descent down the 'road' from Triscombe Stone on a snowy weekend winter patrol. It gets steep very quickly and the first few metres are tarmac, so extremely slippery when covered with packed snow that has effectively become white ice. Chris called me to say that he had slid on the ice and was wedged halfway down Triscombe Quarry road. Damn, that's my weekend off scuppered! I knew that if he was pointing downhill that the only safe way to try and pull him out would be from the top; we didn't want anyone sliding into each other. I pulled up carefully behind his vehicle and got out to assess the precarious situation. As soon as I slammed the door my Land Rover slid on the pack ice by itself for a few metres and gently nudged itself up against the back of Chris's vehicle… snookered! Damn again.

A predicament. We didn't dare go forward because the road only got steeper; we would undoubtedly gain speed and lose control or possibly slide into someone else coming up. We couldn't go back because we would just spin and probably make the frozen road even more polished for a now-necessary double rescue… and anyway, the only reason both vehicles weren't already at the bottom of the hill was because Chris's vehicle was wedged into the bank. Better ring Bill again. Luckily, he lived close by.

Bill turned up in his (now rather familiar) big blue tractor, shook his head and gave us a tut and a wry grin. Weren't we the professionals? Bill did the same as I had; he stopped his vehicle and got out to assess the mess. He put a chain over my tow hitch, nodded and jumped back into his cab. Before he had even managed to select reverse his huge, heavy tractor started to slide slowly forwards on the pack ice. Even Bill now looked rather worried; the weight of his tractor would take all three vehicles down the hill and squash ours to a pulp in the process. The four giant wheels spun backwards on the ice, the tractor stayed in the same spot and we all held our breath… amazingly they slowly started to find traction, and my Land Rover was towed inch by inch (again) back up to flatter ground. He then very carefully did the same with Chris's lighter vehicle and soon we were all home and dry. Phew, that could have been expensive. We definitely owed Bill a pint!

A new Somerset Fire Service Museum was established just outside Bishops Lydeard and I was invited to attend its inaugural opening. We had provided them with some fire-fighting paraphernalia: fire beaters, signs, photographs, etc, and they wanted to thank us. Amazingly, part of the launch celebration was a hot air balloon flight!

I excitedly accepted the invitation. I had never been in a hot air balloon before (I don't suppose many people often get the chance). I was rather surprised at the size of the beautifully made basket; it was huge, and I think that there were at least half a dozen of us who were to take to the skies. I have to say that this was a most wonderful experience: a warm, late summer evening, the verdant landscape accentuated by the lengthening shadows from a slowly setting sun.

We left the waving throng below with a loud roar from the burner. The huge balloon lifted without effort and the ground fell away rapidly below us, quickly revealing the stunning countryside and the sunset-drenched western scarp of the hills. Tiny cars zipped along the grey ribbon of the A358. The gentle south-westerly wind bore us over the southern end of the Quantocks and out across the Levels. What immediately struck me was how quiet it all was; although there was obviously a wind (otherwise we wouldn't be moving), you couldn't hear it or feel it, you were part of it... it was magical. I dared myself to peer directly over the brown suede basket lip, observing the countryside slip away vertically beneath.

As we drifted across the wet meadowlands near Burrow Mump the dark, elongated shadow of the balloon reached horses and cattle before we were overhead, scattering them in a confused, 'eclipse' induced panic. I could imagine how it must feel crossing the plains of the Serengeti or the Maasai

Mara with zebra and wildebeest reacting in exactly the same way to a huge, alien, fire-breathing shadow maker in the sky.

As the red sun sank somewhere into the sea beyond Exmoor a large, yellow Harvest Moon started to rise above the darkening backdrop of the Mendip Hills – the perfect, poetic finale!

All too soon my Somerset Safari was coming to an end, and we landed at dusk in a field at the base of the hills, the basket being bumpily dragged on its side across the wheat stubble for about a hundred metres. Quite a way to end the week! However, another adventure was about to begin, starting with a much longer flight...

It was through my increasing experience and confidence using fire as a management tool and demonstrating our now proven swaling skills to other land managers that I was successful in securing a professional career exchange to the opposite side of the planet.

Chapter Eight: A Land Down Under

I had always wanted to see a bit more of our wonderful world, so I pursued the idea of doing a work exchange with a ranger in another country. Amazingly I got the go-ahead in principle from my employer but had to sort out all the details and travel costs myself. I placed an advert in the International Ranger Federation newsletter and soon heard back from a number of rangers from the Australian National Parks Service. To cut a long story short, April 1997 saw the Russell family flying out to Victoria for a year's exchange. This also entailed a house and car swap; we were doing a whole family/work exchange… quite an adventure.

I managed to get British Airways to fund my flights through their Conservation Award fund. I based my exchange application on fire management, using carefully controlled fires as a valuable tool in heathland restoration and habitat management. This seemed to go down very well as fire management and its control are – unsurprisingly – important land management factors in Australia.

I had never flown further than Finland or southern Europe before, and this flight was going to take twenty-four hours with a brief break in Singapore. To entertain my young daughters (and selfishly to experience it myself) I cheekily asked one of the flight attendants if it would be possible for the captain to show us the cockpit. Rather surprisingly, a few minutes later she came back with a 'Yes, that would be fine, come this way.' We followed her to the front of the plane and were led into the very sanctum of this gigantic flying machine. We stood just behind the two seated pilots, and they turned to welcome us. Both were eating their lunch – they explained that the plane was flying itself on autopilot and very briefly went through the myriad of dials and levers. I'm not too sure about the girls, but I was in awe – this vast, complicated 'airbus' was at that moment flying itself to Australia! The view through the cockpit window was breath-taking; we looked down over thirty thousand feet to the sparkling Indian Ocean and the Bay of Bengal. As far as the eye could see in every direction were brilliant white puffy clouds with their polka-dot shadows dotted across the vast blue world below. This was a privileged experience; you couldn't do that today!

After landing, and rather travel-weary, we headed out of Melbourne, Victoria, into a vast landscape. It felt like we were leaving civilisation behind as we wound our way through the dark, tall eucalyptus forests of the Great Dividing Range, the headlights picking out yellow, diamond-shaped road signs depicting wombats or kangaroos. We eventually arrived at our mud-brick house in the small town of Alexandra in the pitch dark. We woke up the next bright, sunny morning to the unfamiliar, beautiful sounds of Australian bird calls. Rosie and Ellie ran excitedly into our bedroom shouting: 'Mum! Dad! There's monkeys outside!' Not monkeys – just wonderful, unusual (to us) birds.

We excitedly explored our new home. A large shady veranda led onto a long garden with a play area, sweet-smelling eucalypts, and a little creek with a pond at the bottom. It seemed ideal. In the evening the garden was filled with an unusual and exotic high-pitched sound... cicadas? 'Nah, tree frogs, mate,' explained our neighbour. 'Snake food!'... great. As far as I knew we could have one or two living under the veranda – we certainly had a big fluffy possum in the log shed!

I went into town to buy each of us a torch. I had heard about horrible spiders that come into the home as autumn approaches and I didn't want any of us to tread on one in the dark on the way to 'the dunnie'. I parked behind a pick-up truck in the high street and read the bumper sticker a few feet in front of me... 'The Only True Wilderness is between a Greenie's Ears', it read. 'Hmmm... welcome to rural Australia' I thought.

For the next twelve months I was to be Ranger-in-Charge for Fraser National Park, a large lake system and forested hills with house boats and camping grounds a few miles from the town. Also in my jurisdiction was Eildon State Park, a much larger forested and hilly area that stretched towards the central highlands, with the lumpy profile of Mount Buller on the edge of the Australian Alps visible in the distance. The district is known in its Aboriginal name as Murrindindi – Mist of The Mountains.

My first day as an Aussie ranger was quite memorable. I arrived at the park office with my packed lunch, feeling slightly apprehensive as I didn't know anybody, and was quickly greeted with, 'We've got a fire mate, grab some overalls and jump in the truck!' Blimey – I hadn't expected to be fighting bushfires on my first morning!

I reached for a pair of bright green overalls hanging on the wall that looked about my size and started to get into them. To my horror, the biggest, most grotesque spider I have ever seen jumped out of them and scuttled across the floor. I hadn't expected that either... another great welcome to the Land Down Under, I thought!

I jumped into the passenger seat of the 4x4 and we tore off down the dirt track in a cloud of dust towards the smoke. My new work colleague, Katrina Gray, introduced herself to me between the crackling messages coming over the walkie-talkie radio. The fire turned out to be a grass fire in dry farmland just outside the park boundary and we managed to quickly contain it before it had a chance to take hold in the dry brush and forest of the National Park.

We all gathered round for a briefing, and I was soon properly introduced to Brian Boyle, my new boss.

'So how d' ya put out fires back in Pommieland?' he asked with a wry, slightly patronising smile. 'With an old Land Rover mud flap screwed to a hazel stick,' I replied. Not that far wrong really.

Next day there was a liaison meeting with the Natural Resources & Environment team in the Park district offices, shared with their Forestry Department. We were in a large operations room, where one whole wall was covered with a huge map of the area. What struck me immediately was that it was completely opposite to any map you would find in England. Instead of being pretty much white with small pockets of green, this map was almost all green, with small pockets of white. Most of the map showed forest, literally from floor to ceiling. I had never experienced such an environment before; this year was going to be interesting.

Brian was keen to find out whether my off-roading skills were up to scratch, so I described the area that I usually patrolled. "Hmm, ok" he said, "I think you'd better check out some of our area then". We drove out into the Park and into increasingly rugged terrain, steep dry wooded hills with narrow, ridge-top tracks. At the base of one hill, Brian stopped the Hilux, a huge slab of red rock directly ahead. He slammed the 4x4 into low-ratio and differential-lock and the perilous ascent began. I couldn't quite believe it, the vehicle's gnarly tyres gripped and slipped, but we were climbing. Once again, I was looking through a windscreen that only showed blue sky and I felt like an astronaut during take-off. I was relieved when we got to the top of the rocky slope and levelled out onto the ridge.

But the 'roller-coaster' ridge track was barely wider than the vehicle itself and the land dropped away steeply on either side, the bottom of the hill impossible to see through the trees. Brian somehow turned the vehicle around at the end of the spur, in a multiple-point-turn, I could hardly watch, as front bumper and tailgate hung over empty space. Now it was my turn and I cautiously crawled back along the ridge. Skirting large rock outcrops, forcing me even closer to the edge, was nerve racking. Then came the dreaded descent down the rock slab. "Just let the vehicle do the work" Brian calmly directed "and don't use the brakes". I let the nose roll over the edge, my sweating hands gripping the steering wheel for dear life and my right foot instinctively resting on the brake pedal.

"How do you know when a slope's too steep?" I nervously asked. "When ya peelin' ya lips off the windshield" he 'helpfully' replied. Instead of blue sky all I could now see through the screen was the rocky ground coming ever closer, but we made it. I only had to use that track on one more occasion, but this time on a quad bike, which was actually even scarier. I certainly didn't want to stall it on the way up, having to come down backwards was not an option.

I soon had my first taste of experiencing the wonderful wildlife the area could offer, while out on patrol in these extensive forests. Travelling solo into the remote south-eastern area of the Park, I forded a wide river in the Landcruiser and around the next bend, in the middle of the forest track directly ahead, were two huge wedge-tailed eagles. I think they hadn't heard me because the engine noise was muted when I cautiously crossed the river in low gear. They were squabbling over a king brown snake! I was about twenty metres away from them and they still seemed huge – certainly the largest birds I had ever seen and one of the largest eagles in the world, with a wingspan of up to nearly three metres. For a few seconds they were unaware of my presence, engrossed in their activity, but on noticing me one of the birds released its hold on the snake and lifted its heavy bulk into the air on slow, powerful wing beats. The other, not wanting to let go of this hearty meal, launched itself into the sky carrying the long, writhing snake in its talons, and I watched it gradually disappear above the treetops.

Not long afterwards, while quietly walking along a narrow forest trail to check out one of the camping areas (deliberately focusing my attention on the ground after the recent brown snake episode), I suddenly stopped in my tracks – I could feel that something was watching me. I turned my head and stared directly into the banded face of a swamp wallaby some five metres away. I was shocked and enthralled at the same time but didn't know what to do; my first face-to-face encounter with the local wildlife.

Do I stand still, walk slowly backwards, make a noise? The wallaby was upright, as tall as I was... and it just stared back, not fazed by me at all. It was incredibly bulky, hairy and had long claws. Can they be dangerous when disturbed? Do they defend their patch of forest? Do they box? I realised at this point that I did not know how to react or behave when encountering a wild Australian mammal on its home turf.

For a few slow seconds the wallaby stared me down, neither of us moving a muscle, then it turned its head and nonchalantly bounded off, vanishing among the tangle of wattle and gum trees. A rare and unexpected encounter.

I was lucky enough to be starting my exchange at the same time as a ranger from the Auckland Parks & Wildlife Service in New Zealand: Maurice Puckett (his father, it turned out, had been an Olympic runner). I don't think that the Parks Department really knew what to do with us both at first, so we were sent off to experience other parks across the state. Sounded ok to me.

Our initial adventure took us to Wilson's Promontory National Park, in southeast Victoria. The Prom, as it is generally known, is one of Victoria's most popular National Parks and was celebrating its 100th anniversary. Maurice and I were given an initial task of walking out to the famous lighthouse located on a dramatic granite headland, the southernmost tip of the Australian continent – Tasmania next stop! We were to record the state of the walking tracks, way-marking and signage and report back. It was a great feeling to be out on foot in wild Australia, with not a person, road or building in sight... was this actually a job? Was I really here?

Once out on the headland, we sat down to grab a drink and admire the pristine coastal environment, the crystal-clear waters below us punctuated with the wave-splashed domes of huge granite boulders. I gazed at one for a while, just taking in the scene... it looked a bit like the back of a whale. 'Hey Maurice, look there's a whale!' I joked, pointing towards the grey rounded shape. This attracted his attention, and he came to sit next to me, eyes peeled on the rock, but not overly impressed by my humour. But then, from the left, a huge gnarly shape swam towards us in the water directly below the cliff we were sitting on – a humpback whale! It was playing with a huge fur seal, and both were rolling around in the glass-clear water below. I'll never forget that moment looking down at my first ever whale and catching its intelligent, knowing eye. We watched them for a few minutes before they separated, and the whale disappeared into the depths. Did that really just happen, I thought? Again, it struck me – what a fantastic privilege it was to be doing this ranger exchange to the other side of the world, a world so different from the one I had left behind. Later in the year, with the rest of the family, we were lucky enough to watch other whales at The Prom, southern right whales breaching far off the beach, their distinctive flukes silhouetted against the bright blue horizon. It is comforting to think that they're possibly doing that right now, all those oceans away, as I write. Thankfully, whale numbers are now recovering well from being hunted to near extinction almost 100 years ago... we're doing something right at last.

Maurice and I had other adventures too. During the winter we checked cross-country ski routes and alpine vegetation erosion at Mount Buffalo National Park in the western end of the Alps. This is a truly amazing, elevated landscape, quite literally an 'island in the sky' with deep-blue alpine skies and giant snow-topped granite boulders towering above beautiful, hardy and twisted snow gums. We stayed in the

Ranger Station, and I was surprised at how cold Australia could get: a night-time minus 10 degrees, the thermometer read. I was so overawed with this place that I managed to bring my family back a few weeks later for a short break. Skiing in Australia was not something that any of us had seriously thought we would be doing!

We hired our equipment and set off for the slopes (well, the slope). Mount Buffalo isn't the biggest of ski resorts, but perfect for introducing the sport to our two young daughters. After a few practice runs Jilly asked if I wouldn't mind keeping an eye on the girls so that she could go and ski by herself for a few minutes. 'Yeah sure, don't worry, they'll be fine with me,' I said.

As Jill passed over the top of us on the ski lift moments later, helpless to assist, she could see Rosie being transported by a paramedic on his snowmobile and me rescuing Ellie from the bottom of the slope. In the time it had taken Jill to queue for the chair lift, Rosie's skis had crossed and she had fallen over on the aptly named drag lift, been dragged along the snow as the wire stretched, smacked on the head by the seat as it rapidly recoiled, been hit in the back from behind by a snowboarder and turned the snow pink with her blood. In panic, Ellie had let go of the drag lift and had slid down the ski slope backwards. Quite a scene.

We all ended up at the ski medical centre and Rosie was given oxygen. They were worried about her head injury due to the velocity of the impact and called for the helicopter to come and take her off the mountain to hospital. But by this time the weather had closed in, and the helicopter had to be stood down. 'She'll have to go to hospital by car. You got a four-wheel drive?' the paramedic asked. I explained that there was a spare ranger truck I could use. 'Keep her awake, don't let her fall asleep.' We phoned the hospital in Bright and they said they'd be expecting us. It was a long way down the mountain; it was going to take about an hour.

We all piled into the 4x4 and focused on keeping Rosie awake. Off we sped, for about a hundred metres. 'Damn, I can't believe it, it's got a flat!' Back to base, all piled into the family car, luckily still with its snow chains on. Halfway down the mountain the snow changed to tarmac, off with the snow chains and carry on down the twisting roads. Civilisation at last, straight to the Medical Centre, to find a note on the door: 'Gone to tea. Back in an hour.' Really? Rosie was getting very sleepy by now. Phew, a café. An hour later, all fed and watered, back to the doctor, who checked her head and pupil sizes. 'Well, she's got through the critical bit, she'll be right.' That was it. Back up the mountain, on with the snow chains. Quite a day. Next morning, all bandaged up and looking like an Egyptian mummy, Rosie was bravely back on the slopes, bless her.

In the spring, Maurice and I helped with surveys of the rare and elusive rock wallaby amongst the strange rocky landscapes of the Grampians National Park in the southwest of the state. This is one of the richest Aboriginal art sites in southeast Australia and the views from The Pinnacle look-out of the forests, sandstone mountain ranges and surrounding plains are still memorable. Huge, highly vocal flocks of brilliant white sulphur crested cockatoos were regular and mesmerising intrusions to the vast blue green of the forest. Towards the end of the exchange, I was invited to give a talk to the Parks Victoria annual conference in Halls Gap (with hotel accommodation and provided with a smart Government car), so I took the family along for a much-needed road trip to this wonderful part of western Victoria.

We undertook nocturnal surveys amongst the towering mountain ash and cool-temperate forests of Lake Mountain in the Yarra Ranges looking for signs of Leadbeater's possum. This adorable little possum, thought to be extinct until rediscovery in 1961, is a crucial species to conserve and to help heighten the public's awareness of the plight of Victoria's old-growth forests from overzealous logging and wildfire. The mountain ash is the world's tallest flowering tree and a scenic drive along the nearby Black Spur through these majestic trees and lush, primeval tree ferns feels like entering a real Jurassic Park.

Maurice and I did our firefighting and boat-handling courses together and relocated over-populating koalas from Snake Island in the Nooramunga Marine and Coastal Park. Koalas had been naively moved to the island in the 1930s as their mainland habitats were being grubbed out for farming land. With no natural predators their population had grown so large that they were now destroying the place and running out of their sole food source of eucalyptus leaves.

Our job was to catch and return as many as possible to suitable habitats back on the mainland. My role, as a nimble tree climber (and extremely gullible 'Pom') was to lasso the koalas up in the tree canopy and lower them down to the (more sensible) rangers below. Here they were covered with a hessian sack, weighed, sexed and their health details recorded. They were then carefully put in individual wooden boxes for transport.

Lassoing koalas twenty feet or so up a gum tree is not particularly easy, but I soon mastered the task. That is, until I had a very angry adult male to deal with. He was twisting and spinning as I lowered him with the pole lasso, spitting and grunting like a good 'un. Once lowered to the ground he quickly exploded from the sack and headed straight back up the tree, shredding bark and ripping timber in his fury with talon-like claws. I was attached to the tree trunk with climbing ropes and carabiners, unable to get out of his way. 'Don't let him get near ya, he'll rip ya!' came the warning from below. Great. The only thing I could do was keep my boot on top of his head until he climbed round the other side of the tree and disappeared up into the canopy, spitting and hissing with rage. Wow, they're not quite as cuddly as I'd thought!

My colleagues below looked up at me from under the rims of their iconic Akubra ranger hats, wiping themselves dry – they were now covered in koala pee! 'What a little stinker! Smoko time I reckon,' said Sandy Brown the project manager. Too right, I thought.

Maurice and I helped construct a timber suspension bridge across the river in the rugged Cathedral Ranges State Park and I had the pleasure of spending time deep in the Dividing Range forests of the Blue and Black Ranges with 'The Dogger'.

The dogger's job was to kill wild dogs and European foxes. Packs of feral dogs and lone foxes roamed the forest and preyed on unsuspecting Australian wildlife and occasionally attacked livestock outside the Park. The dogger was employed to find out where these carnivores were and to poison them and shoot them if he could. I'm not sure that I felt entirely comfortable accompanying him on these trips, but he was certainly a character, a real bushman. He knew the remotest parts of forest like no one else, spending all of his working days away from other human beings under its blue-green, aromatic roof.

Being used to working closely with the forestry guys back home I asked if I could spend some time with the foresters here to get to know how they managed these vast forests, and to my surprise was told that I was the first 'Parkie' to have ever requested this. It seemed that there had always been a bit of a 'them and us' between the National Parks and the State Forest staff. Many of the Parks staff seemed to be young graduates from 'the city', while the foresters were mainly older and more local.

I was given permission to do this and was allocated time with 'Buffer', the District Forest Officer. He had spent his whole working career in this 'neck of the woods' and took great pride in showing me around this mountainous forest district.

He introduced me to some pretty tough woodsmen (all with checked shirts with ripped-off sleeves, naturally). I was shocked at the extent of hardwood clear-fell and the burning of debris; this was forestry on a huge scale. The only bits of wild-ish forest left untouched were narrow strips along stream and riverbanks (to minimise erosion) and the fenced-off water catchment areas that fed an increasingly thirsty Melbourne to the south.

One of our family friends in Alexandra was the District's Fire Officer, John Hopper or 'Hops', as he was known. We were both interested in fire management, using fire as a tool and how to deal with wildfires. In the hot, dry Australian summer his role was crucial to the protection of forests, farmland and communities. He was constantly checking conditions, soil dryness indexes, wind and weather forecasts and was on constant standby to direct bushfire management across the whole North District. Much of his observation was done from the air and he invited me out to fly over the area and to take part in wildfire control practices. The summer that I was in Victoria was one of the El Niño years; very hot, very dry and potentially disastrous for bushfires.

Seeing the land from the cockpit of a small plane was a wonderful experience. A crumpled landscape of forested mountains as far as the eye could see, with occasional yellowed paddocks and farmsteads in between... no wonder they took fire management so seriously. How on earth would you stop a forest fire in this wild and woolly terrain, with a hot desert wind blowing from the north? It made managing heathland fires on the Quantocks look like child's play.

Before our exchange was over, we were lucky enough to have a couple of summer breaks down at Port Fairy, at the western end of the Great Ocean Road. One of my father's old university friends had done rather well for himself (as CEO for Glaxo Australasia) and had some holiday property he let us use. The journey down the Great Ocean Road from Melbourne was stunning and we enjoyed being tourists, stopping off at Apollo Bay in the Otways National Park and visiting the iconic Twelve Apostilles on the dramatic Port Campbell National Park coast. And on good advice from friends Mike and Ollie Wellings in Wonthaggi we thoroughly enjoyed Port Fairy's popular international folk festival.

We had a forced stop at Torquay on the way back as the outside temperature had reached a very uncomfortable 42 degrees. Our 'exchange car' had no air-conditioning so we cooled down in one of the huge surf shops, making use of their air-con and chilled water cooler. When we had recovered a bit and walked back outside half an hour later the temperature had dropped to a more manageable 26 degrees. The air was now coming off the cold, moist Southern Ocean instead of the continent's hot, dry interior. I had experienced minus 10 degrees at Mount Buffalo, and we had just been in plus 42... more than 50 degrees difference.

Watching the news back in the UK in 2009 I was shocked to see that Marysville, one of the local towns we knew well and whose popular old-fashioned tearoom we enjoyed visiting, was burnt to the ground and thirty-four people lost their lives in the horrendous Black Saturday Bushfires. This was dreadful to see and really brought home how serious an issue it is out there. Climate change and increasing global warming isn't going to help; the last decade has been the hottest on record. July 2022 saw the highest temperatures ever recorded in the UK, over 40 degrees C, and an official drought. A stark indication of things to come?

In 2003, a few years after returning from Australia I was asked to present a talk at the 4th World Ranger Congress at Wilsons Promontory National Park; the theme was 'Engaging Local Communities'. This is something we generally do very well in the UK as all our National Parks and AONBs are home to communities – and had been for hundreds of years before our Parks were designated back in the 1950s. Most Parks in Australia had no towns or villages, and so many of the rangers had limited experience engaging with residents. It was great to be back in such a stunning place and catching up with old colleagues.

One of our site visits was to the southern end of the Park and I was able to re-tread the wonderful walking track with its winding boardwalk between Tidal River and the brilliant, white sands and clear blue water of Waterloo Bay. Seeing the impressive and rare red-tailed black cockatoos with their distinctive head crests flying amongst the trees was an extra treat. We were picked up by boat and during our return journey were able to observe the beaches, granite-studded hills and lush forests of this remote and pristine part of the Park from out at sea. A once-in-a-lifetime experience.

I was worried for a while, though, when I noticed a horrible boil on my foot. I thought it could be a white-tail spider bite; they can be particularly nasty, and I didn't fancy skin necrosis. I had one of the Aussie rangers check it for me. 'Nah, it's just a blister mate!' I felt like a whinging Pom.

Part of the congress experience included the opportunity to work-shadow an Australian ranger for a week. I was lucky enough to know one very well. Bill Gurnett the ex-Head Ranger from Exmoor National Park, had done a similar work exchange to me but had decided to stay. I stayed with him and his family and he showed me around the less-visited parts on the eastern side of the Park via barrier gates accessible to Management Vehicles Only. From a vantage point amongst scattered banksia trees, I gazed across the protected bay of Corner Inlet to Snake Island in the distance – happy memories!

The flight back home was memorable as the plane chased the setting sun for what seemed hours across this incredible continent, and I enjoyed observing the country slowly slipping into the blackness of evening below: the Great Australian Bight, the expanse and giant ripples of the Simpson Desert and the beehive-shaped hills of the Bungle Bungle ranges. Wearing a face mask throughout the twenty-four-hour flight back due to the SARS epidemic wasn't quite so much fun, though. Who'd have thought we'd all be wearing them again nearly twenty years later!

Chapter Nine: Protected Landscape

Working for a county council did seem rather sensible and grown-up at times. Most of the male employees wore suits and ties – we didn't. Chris and I liked to be a bit irreverent; we were still in our early thirties and (although conscientious and committed) believed work to be enjoyed wherever possible. We loved driving through the centre of Taunton in a big green, mud-splattered Land Rover and parking it in front of County Hall. I guess we liked to let people working there know that we still existed.

One hot summer's day we were severely reprimanded on our way into C Block, where the planning department and our bosses were based. 'You can't go in there looking like that!' snapped the grey-suited, middle-aged planning officer. 'Looking like what?' we quizzed, somewhat flummoxed. 'You're wearing shorts!' Good grief!

Quarterly Quantock Joint Advisory Committee meetings were held on Friday afternoons. These were very important meetings at which we had to present our reports on issues such as practical work, visitor management, volunteer wardens, landowner and user group liaison, etc.

My first committee report expressed my utter shock at the dreadful state of the hills due to vehicle damage. I was familiar with the Shropshire Hills where you could walk for miles without seeing a vehicle let alone any damage; and anyway, I was in post to protect the hills. I had naively and inadvertently let slip my dislike of the hunt's activities (who had a large, motorised following). It did seem that if you weren't with them, you were against them. This was always a tricky subject because no one could really deny or condone this damage, but it could all get very sensitive and political. The stag-hunting issue was always going to be the elephant in the room – for most of us, anyway.

Our committee was made up of three elected members from each of the districts that covered the hills and three Somerset county councillors, along with official Government representatives from English Nature, the Countryside Commission and Forestry Commission. Fortunately, my boss Ken was an expert in political savvy, diplomacy and astuteness – he knew how to play their games. He never lost his temper and always stayed calm and cool, unlike some in the room. He always had the perfect answer to probing or uncomfortable questions about how much the warden service was costing or why both wardens needed a vehicle.

He was the perfect boss; calm, supportive, patient, intelligent and well respected. It's from him I learnt when to bite my tongue if the politics got a little testing!

Due to the continual hard work by Ken (and others) in convincing the Government that AONBs were important, they were at last beginning to get better funding. We were now an AONB Service and had the opportunity to increase our team. Chris had become AONB Manager, I was now Senior Ranger and had a new ranger in tow, Andy Harris from Bishops Lydeard. Andy and his friend had been visiting the hills for a while in his old blue Land Rover, parking at Lydeard Hill car park in the evenings to watch the deer. I didn't know who owned this vehicle and had become rather suspicious of its regular nocturnal parking, wrongly assuming that it could belong to a new poacher in the neighbourhood. How wrong I was.

Andy soon became a most valued and conscientious member of the team and a close friend. He and I both received honorariums from the council for one hundred days continuous cover during the Foot and Mouth epidemic in 2001. Disinfectant mats at all cattlegrids onto the open hill had to be sprayed at least twice daily, miles of stock proofing around the whole of the commons checked, the public had to be advised on changing situations and any ensuing problems dealt with. Andy had excellent ornithological and local knowledge and we had many adventures, mainly involving poaching patrols, quad bikes and Exmoor Ponies.

Just parking the quad bike was usually a bit of an adventure whenever I was involved. Its (rather sensitive) throttle was a small lever operated by the thumb on your right hand – what could be simpler? I pulled the bike up in front of the office, outside a window, smiled at a group of people having a meeting inside and attempted to reverse into a parking space, all the while being watched. As I selected reverse (not all that easy) and twisted the handlebars to the left, my thumb pressed even harder on the throttle and I flew backwards up the bank, disappearing through the privet hedge... not cool. Further incidents involving this hair-trigger throttle occurred on at least two more occasions as I tried to park the quad bike behind the flail on top of our big trailer. The first time the quad bike and I mounted the flail and almost entered the opened back window of the Toyota Hilux, much to the horror of Andy's two flat-coated retrievers inside. The second occasion I was left clinging to the handlebars of a high-revving, totally vertical quad bike having done the same thing! However, it was an essential tool for checking on the Exmoor Ponies when we had deep snow. It was also a lot of fun, smashing through the powdery snow drifts up at Birches Corner and Cothelstone Hill.

The pony herd is a 'working herd'. Their job is to graze and browse the vegetation, helping to maintain the important rough grassland and scattered scrub habitat, a place where glow worms can still be found, kestrels hover and cuckoos perch in the old hawthorns. We brought the fifteen ponies over from Exmoor National Park in 1992, purebred, rarer than giant pandas and now being used increasingly in nature conservation schemes throughout the country. This was the first time for hundreds of years that a wild herd of Exmoors had the freedom to roam the Quantock summits, and 'bringing them back' was a very special moment for us. They are basically our native horse, perfectly evolved to survive our wet, windy and often cold climate. We had originally thought of using sheep to graze this hilltop, but too many dog walkers prevented this idea; to an Exmoor Pony's ancient DNA memory bank a dog is a wolf, so they avoid them or just stand firm as a tough posse and stare them out. They've also got a pretty hefty kick if needed!

We came to have huge respect for this handsome herd and checking up on them was a daily responsibility, shared between Andy, myself and key volunteers. Occasionally the ponies would have to be rounded-up and held in the corral when welfare checking or veterinary services were required. Two funny incidents spring to mind. The first was when I was dragged around the corral on my belly, lassoed to a very strong foal, before an audience of visiting conservation volunteers sitting along the fence; a scene from a Thelwell rodeo, which resulted in very sore ribs. The second involved Simon (our main pony checker), who was assisting us when having a colt castrated. The vet had administered a strong sedative (Immobilon), and the deed was quickly done. A second drug wakes the pony up. This happened so rapidly that Simon (an ex-Yorkshire miner) was thrown into the air and across the corral as the very disgruntled animal sprang to life again!

We soon learned from bitter experience that even the young ponies were surprisingly strong!

As rangers we worked closely with police officers to try and deal with all sorts of rural and urban-fringe crime. Illegal off-roading, deer poaching, badger digging, wildlife poisoning, fly-tipping, car crime to name but a few. We also assisted in occasional search and rescue incidents, looking for missing persons. It was quite clear that we could do with our own Police Community Support Officer (PCSO) to cover the Quantock area specifically as it was pretty awkward dealing with three different police districts. This idea was taken up, funding found, and we eventually got our very own PCSO to cover the AONB. This was the first partnership of its kind in the country and generated some excellent PR for all concerned. Unfortunately, the advert for the job only attracted one person. I happened to be on holiday in Portugal during this initial part of the recruitment process and would have been happier for a re-advertisement of the post to get a wider choice of interviewees.

On my return I learnt that Shaun (an ex-security guard) had been appointed. He proudly appeared at the ranger's office in Nether Stowey in his smart new uniform and shiny, yellow and blue Nissan Patrol. We soon got to like Shaun; he was particularly amiable and had a great sense of humour. However, he would regularly lose his police notebook (a serious no no), he spent a lot of time chatting in the office, drinking our coffee and (more importantly) munching through our custard creams. We had to keep subtly suggesting to him that perhaps he ought to go out on patrol!

He was extremely keen to use his four-wheel drive to its best advantage but was told that he couldn't go off-road until he'd passed his off-road driving instruction. We had a course arranged, only two weeks away. We'd been having regular illegal motorbike problems in the Bicknoller area: 'Whatever you do, don't follow the bikes down Bicknoller Combe' we told him.

We soon had a rather panicky phone call from him. He had attempted to drive down the combe and got his new vehicle wedged up against a tree at the bottom. Retrieving his truck was not easy, his supervisor was not overly impressed, and the repairs were very expensive. 'Right, whatever you do, don't be tempted to go off-road until after your course!' However, another phone call, this time from Bill Fewings (yes – the one with the tractor): 'I've just had to tow Shaun's 4x4 up out of Quantock Combe on its roof.' He had attempted a very steep, rocky track that led down into the forest; apparently, on leaning over to get something from his briefcase on the back seat (not a good idea), he had lost control and his newly repaired truck had careered down the combe on its side. Bill could only tow it back out on its roof!

After that Shaun was barred from using a four-wheel drive and 'patrolled' the hills in a Vauxhall Astra. He sometimes rode shotgun with us in our Land Rovers, having a uniformed representative of the Avon and Somerset Constabulary assist with cocky, illegal off-roaders was most helpful!

My last journey with him was quite memorable, cutting dangerous bends on the wrong side of the road with his windscreen wipers on full pelt, but no rain!

The partnership project soon came to an end and wasn't continued. This was a great shame as the idea had much potential and we had fought very hard to make it happen.

Various district PCSOs would occasionally drop into our office (now at Fyne Court) to 'chew the cud', drink coffee and (yes) munch custard creams... we would pass useful information back and forth, mostly to do with burnt-out cars, car break-ins, fly-tipping and suspected deer poachers. One day the Bridgwater Area PCSO rang the office to say that she had a suspected bird of prey poisoning incident and asked if she could bring the bird in for proper identification. She knocked at the office door, and I went out to meet her. She had a big black rubbish bag tied at the top. 'It's in here,' she said. I opened the bag, peered inside and to my surprise found that this particular 'buzzard' had a large yellow bill and bright orange, webbed feet! It still makes me laugh to think about it even now.

On the southwest side of the Quantocks is an old quarry site. When I first started working on the hills it was still active with large, noisy machinery and constant lorry traffic creating dust and disturbance through the tiny hamlet of Triscombe. It was a huge pink gash on the landscape and seemed to be gnawing its way into the very backbone of the hills. It always felt inappropriate in the otherwise beautiful setting of the western scarp, a huge scar in a nationally protected landscape.

In the mid-1990s the quarry company was late in applying for permission to extend their mineral extraction licence, and this gave the county council a legitimate excuse to refuse... which to their credit, they did.

The heavy quarrying plant was all removed, a lake created, and many native trees were planted. We managed to stop the company planting Himalayan balsam; a non-native that would have run rampant to the detriment of native vegetation. Ravens soon established themselves on the cliff face and not long after peregrine falcons also took up residence. Due to their rather noisy shrieking the birds soon attracted interest, but not always from the right people. We were alerted to the fact that a well-known collector was on the look-out for eggs or chicks to sell to Saudi Arabia. So, with the help of the Mendip Hills Search and Rescue Team the chicks were taken out of their nest, brought up to the top, micro-chipped by experts (from the Wildlife Crime Unit) and quickly returned to the nest. If anything was to happen to them at least they could now be tracked and identified.

I was often shocked at the blatant persecution of birds of prey, particularly buzzards, and had to send a number of poisoned carcasses off to be tested. A rabbit carcass was found pegged to the ground, its chest full of blue poison pellets for birds of prey to feed on; indiscriminate poisoning that could have killed anything – buzzard, fox, badger or a walker's pet dog. We worked closely with the police and regularly ran Wildlife

Law training seminars for fellow wardens and police officers. These training days proved to be much valued and well attended; the pleasant, cosy venue of medieval Halsway Manor with its roaring log fire and wonderful sandwiches, tea and cake only added to a great day.

One of the main topics covered was the laws (or lack of them) related to deer poaching. The Quantocks and Exmoor have significant numbers of wild red deer and these large beasts can be easy pickings for would-be poachers. Poaching has been a feature of the area for centuries, historically, the stealing of the occasional deer for a poor family's table. However, in more recent times it is all about money rather than survival and has no romanticism attached to it.

Venison is classed as game and not meat, so does not have the same thorough checks on food hygiene. A dead deer that has been thrown into the back of a filthy pick-up, dragged across a farmyard and hung up in some grubby old barn can end up cheek-by-jowl next to a piece of prime steak. The Deer Act law relating to poaching basically requires a police officer to have witnessed the event, the poacher to literally have been caught in the act... not very likely. More straightforward and harder-hitting legislation relates to trespass with a firearm, and this is where we focused our attention.

We organised regular night patrols with our local police officers and were occasionally able to get support from the firearms response unit based in Bristol, who would occasionally come down with their multi-bags of Mars Bars, cans of Coca Cola and even a TV in their van! The Royal

Marines also assisted us and enjoyed these 'nocturnal training opportunities' as they could try out their latest night vision binoculars and gun scopes. However, most of the time it was just Chris and I and out on cold, dark winter nights.

We very nearly caught our regular poacher from Holford. We waited (with a police officer), hidden in the bracken, for him to return to pick up a gutted stag that he had shot early that morning. He popped his head above the bracken after a while and cheekily chirped, 'Good morning chaps. Fancy seeing you lot 'ere!' Chris bumped into him on a future poaching patrol, and he proudly boasted that he shot fifty deer a year. One a week sounded quite an exaggeration, but as he always carried a long gutting knife and had been done for GBH, it wasn't sensible to argue too much – he was a little unhinged!

We were genuinely able to report back to our committee that since we were often out and about this was useful PR and was often picked up by the press. Along with local radio and television reports we did a couple of pieces for BBC *Countryfile.* On one occasion John Craven knelt next to a freshly poached deer carcass in Shervage Wood near Holford and cringingly said 'Oh dear, oh dear' in his piece to camera! We weren't entirely sure whether he actually realised what he had said. In honesty, most deer were shot by farmers illegally at night on their own land, so no trespass with firearm laws were being broken. One notorious farmer we knew planted strips of swedes along woodland edges to entice the deer out onto his fields. The corrugated roofs of his farm buildings were littered with the antlered skulls of numerous stags, a simple but crude message to show off his blatant disregard for the local wildlife and any rule of law.

Colleagues you can trust are essential when you're out on your lonesome or just need someone sympathetic to off-load some of the stresses and strains of the job to. I was extremely lucky in having such work mates, including Tim Beazley, the National Trust Warden. Tim was responsible for the Trust's land and was their first Quantock Warden. He was given an ancient green-and-cream-coloured Land Rover and loved to bump his away across the hilltops, accompanied by his faithful dog. Tim became a valuable extra pair of hands, particularly with the swaling work, and helped to develop a closer working relationship with the National Trust. We developed a great friendship over a couple of decades, both being tree lovers. He was a bit of an old hippy at heart and loved his seventies' rock music which would be blaring out from his very chilled-out 'office' whenever I would turn up for a chat. 'Proper coffee' with warm milk or 'posh tea' was made on the wood-fired Rayburn and meetings were held sitting in his very homely, slightly smoky kitchen ... aah, those were the days!

Tim sadly passed away recently at his home in Brittany. Old colleagues and I from his Quantock days planted an oak tree in his memory at Fyne Court. A long-lived, living legacy for a genuinely nice guy. Late one evening, driving back from a meeting at Tim's place, something happened that I will never forget. I still can't quite believe it happened and haven't mentioned it to too many people.

On the wooded section of road below Cothelstone Hill, the Land Rover headlights picked up an unusual shape crossing the road from right to left about ten metres in front of me: a big cat! My brain tried to register it; not a deer, not a dog – the head was too rounded, the body too muscular and low – and a long, curved tail. It then melted into the darkness, it was at least a metre and a half long and beige coloured: a puma. I had seen deer and dogs almost daily on the Quantocks – I knew their shape and manner – but this was neither, a totally different creature. There were other big cat sightings from time to time; a farmer in Plainsfield told me that he had seen one effortlessly clear a six-foot fence; police officers mentioned that colleagues occasionally reported sightings during their night patrols; and two days after my experience a father rang the office to say that he and his son had been petrified hearing strange, deep guttural sounds in the woods near Birches Corner (close to my sighting). I kept my brief encounter quiet; the last thing I wanted was any media attention attracting madcap trophy hunters with high-velocity rifles stalking the woods, and anyway most wild creatures sensibly avoid humans.

However, for a while it did feel quite strange whenever I was out on foot by myself in the woods…

Around this time, I attended a search and rescue training course for rangers hosted by Exmoor National Park. It was held at Pinkery Farm, an outdoor education centre managed by Somerset County Council in the remote area of the moor called The Chains close to where Devon and Somerset meet.

Part of the training 'experience' was to spend a night out alone on the moors in a bivvy bag.

The other participants refused to do this, 'couldn't see the point' apparently; I wasn't overly impressed.

I trudged out onto the moor, heading to the watershed of this open landscape where any rain falling will either travel all the way to the English Channel in the south or tumble rapidly north to the Bristol Channel. I settled down for the night, tried to make myself comfortable among the tussocks of Molinia grass and awaited the silent darkness. I must admit, the recent sighting of the big cat on the Quantocks annoyingly allowed thoughts of the Exmoor Beast to slip into my mind. I was alone in the wilds.

As the natural light faded, the electric light pollution of South Wales grew brighter but so too did the myriad of stars that began to fill the sky above me. The seemingly endless display of the Milky Way was phenomenal; the almost total silence (apart from the gentle wind playing in the swaying grasses) was magical and soothing. I don't think that I really got much sleep, but I was captivated by the sight of the slowly revolving heavens, in what is now a designated Dark Skies Area.

I will always remember that night on The Chains, just being out there alone and ambling back to the centre with the rising sun for a warming mug of tea and a comforting bowl of creamy porridge.

Stunning sunrises and atmospheric misty mornings were often enjoyed during the annual deer count. One of the roles of the newly formed Deer Management and Conservation Group was to collate annual figures of the deer population throughout the AONB. With no natural predators left (wolf and bear) deer numbers can escalate out of control and put pressure on farm crops, young trees and the important semi-natural habitat of the Quantock heathland and ancient woodlands. There were wildly varying views on what the deer numbers were, from around 150 to 1000, depending on who you spoke to. Some members of the hunt said 150 (possibly trying to help justify their role or relevance in controlling the numbers); a wheat or beet farmer suffering damaged crops on the hill fringes might put the number closer to 1000.

To settle this difference of opinion regarding deer numbers, and to propose a more scientific and accountable cull, a proper annual count was planned, with much scepticism from certain quarters. No one legally owns the deer until they are dead, at which point they become the property of the landowner. Any culling that had already taken place was *ad hoc*; the hunt took deer; farmers, private estate owners and the Forestry Commission shot deer – and no one was really letting on who shot what.

'You'll never get the exact number' some would say. No, the exact number was not the idea or the aim, but the annual pattern of fluctuations in population and ratio of the sexes was.

A system was devised where volunteers (mainly people interested in deer and who knew the hills) were each given a specific area to cover. It wasn't that difficult finding willing volunteers as the number of people who are infatuated or obsessed with red deer is quite a revelation.

Some will crawl around in camouflage observing stags for months to get the perfect 'Monarch of The Glen' photo or to make sure that they are the first to pick up any discarded antlers in the spring, to add to already large collections which are proudly exhibited on trellis tables at local summer shows.

The northern half of the hills was supervised by the Forestry Commission ranger, and we organised the count in the southern half, each being roughly twenty square miles. Stags, hinds, followers (calves) and any other deer species seen were to be counted. It very soon became apparent that the population ranged from around 650 to 800 deer every year. Numbers of red deer counted over the last thirty years have fluctuated between a low of 306 and high of 958, but in most years, figures have been between 500 to 800.

I must admit that taking part in this every year on the first Sunday in March (weather permitting) was really quite enjoyable. However, getting up around 5am to make a flask of tea, have breakfast and get to Lydeard Hill car park for 6am to start handing out maps in the cold and dark wasn't always that easy. By the time I had handed out the last of the sector maps around 7am and the early spring sun had begun to light up the surrounding countryside I could go and survey my area, which was usually Aisholt Wood.

I think that initially I resented having to be so involved in the organisation of the volunteers and having a limited amount of actual time out counting. I would have loved to have had one of the areas that included the higher ground and enjoyed a good old stroll over the hills at such a special time of day, but I gradually began to love my annual early-morning, quiet creep through this lovely wood.

The wood is owned by the Somerset Wildlife Trust, a remnant of ancient woodland lying between the pretty hamlet of Aisholt (named from its position in or near an ash wood) and Hawkridge Reservoir on the eastern side of the hills.

The beauty of this wood is that it is a mini wilderness. Huge, fallen trees with tangled branches, dense thickets and secret, sunlit glades; this is what a natural woodland should look like. It is an excellent example of the wildlife diversity that will accumulate if a woodland is given a chance to develop in its own natural way. The deep leaf litter, branches and twigs carpeting the woodland floor make it hard for humans to get about but provide a wonderful refuge for the resident wildlife.

My circular route would take about an hour and a half. I would very quietly walk down into the woodland via an old sunken lane, clothed in ferns and primroses, cross the stream in the valley bottom and enter the wood through its nature reserve entrance. Once in the wood, I had to take time to acclimatise and get in 'the zone', treading very carefully as a snapping twig would alert any deer to my presence, and keeping myself downwind as far as possible. Disturbing any birds, such as wrens or blackbirds into making their warning calls, would also alert the wary deer. When you see deer in the woods, they are constantly checking their environment for any tell-tale sound or smell of potential predators.

I would then quietly climb up amongst the ivy-draped oaks to the eastern boundary, allowing me stunning views down the reservoir and out across the misty Somerset Levels.

This was one of my favourite spots and I would often pause here for a few moments to soak up the early morning sunshine and admire the serenity of the quietly waking world below. Water vapour rising in swirling, golden wisps above the reservoir, the steaming breath and bodies of the slowly warming, rugged-up horses in the paddocks and the long-horned, shaggy Highland cattle grazing across the valley. I then climbed carefully back over the rickety fence and into the depths of the wood, checking the badger setts for any fresh signs of illegal disturbance and headed towards Aisholt church.

I briefly emerged from the wood at the western end to admire the setting of this pretty little church against the backdrop of Aisholt Common with its honey-brown bracken and scattered dark-green hollies and the heathy summit of Wills Neck rising above it. Then back into the denser part of the wood on the steep valley side, where I usually spotted the deer, to work my way as quietly as possible down the valley and back to the entrance. I usually counted about ten to fifteen deer, although I probably missed a few hidden amongst the trees; I think they felt pretty safe in there.

We talk a lot about the importance of mindfulness nowadays, and it is undeniably good for the soul. Being in that wood once a year in early spring, focusing on not being noticed, as quiet as a woodland mouse, was a wonderfully grounding experience, a total switch-off from the stresses and strains of everyday life. Walking stealthily alone and picking my way carefully through that tangled, timeless, mossy wood with all my senses heightened and alert in search of wild deer would make me think how it might have been for our ancestors having to hunt for survival in the wild wood of Britain thousands of years ago, using their honed skills and intimate knowledge of their environment and intended quarry. Not a meagre forty-acre woodland like this one, but one that pretty much covered the whole land. In the next little valley or glade, where I was hoping to spot a few deer, they might have come across a wide-horned auroch, a tusked boar, a lolloping brown bear, a protective bison with her calf or a pack of hungry wolves.

Yet again, it was a rare chance to let my imagination run wild and to appreciate being completely absorbed in nature's sylvan embrace, far away from the madding crowd.

Our woodlands are isolated fragments of what used to be – thank goodness for even the smallest of remnants, helping to keep our native ecological gene pool alive. As the UK is so ecologically depleted, joining these islands together is a vital part of rewilding our not-so-wild land.

I studied woodland conservation as part of my degree and my dissertation was based on dating ancient woodland in the

Shropshire Hills using floral indicator species and old maps. I spent many hours in Shrewsbury library looking through the archives and enjoyed passing by Darwin's seated statue, a reminder from the past of how important the study of the natural world is for its future protection. In the region around the Forest of Mortimer much of the woodland was cleared to rid the area of wolves and take away their last Marches sanctuary when the expanding wool industry brought much wealth to the country. The only good wolf in medieval England was a dead one, and much of our folklore was based on vilifying these wonderful beasts; the evil, fanged enemy that needed to be annihilated.

We had a 'Peter and The Wolf' record when I was a boy. I loved Sergei Prokofiev's introduction of different instruments representing the characters: bird – flute, cat – clarinet, duck – oboe, Peter's grandfather – bassoon, wolf – horns; hunters – percussion (which he composed to encourage young children to cultivate an interest in music). However, I always felt sad when the wolf was slain, and the hunters triumphantly carried the wonderful beast back to the village hanging from a pole. It didn't seem like a great story to me.

Chapter Ten: The Gravediggers

I have always been interested in history as well as natural history and teenage explorations of the hillforts, abandoned castles and dykes along the Welsh border encouraged this further. I have been extremely fortunate in being able to develop this interest throughout my career, particularly working closely with archaeologists in the Quantocks and more recently on Dartmoor. Both areas have hugely important historic landscapes, remnants of Bronze Age and Iron Age impacts on the environment: burial cairns, hillforts, standing stones, stone rows, hut circles and earth bank features being the most obvious.

Over the last couple of decades very watchable and informative programmes such as *Time Team* and, more recently, Professor Alice Roberts's *Digging for Britain* have helped bring the fascination of archaeology into the homes of millions of people. The charming BBC TV series *Detectorists* has opened up the joys of metal detecting to many and popular, informative books such as *Mudlarking* by Lara Maiklem recognise the growing popularity of people just going out and discovering history in their own backyard.

I soon became involved with the archaeologists on the Quantocks, and I remember my boss saying 'Aah, you're out with the gravediggers again!'… for a few seconds I didn't really get what he meant, but the penny dropped, and the term stuck. I was to spend many enjoyable days out on the hills helping to record and protect prehistoric features from damage (particularly from erosion and vehicle damage) and gradually increased my knowledge of archaeology in general. The more I got to learn about it the more I wished I'd somehow managed to incorporate it into my degree; but it's never too late to learn! Almost all our landscapes in Britain have remnants or signs of human interaction; our countryside has been shaped by human activity over millennia. You've just got to look for those tell-tale lumps and bumps and bits of old pottery.

The 'historic landscape' of the Quantock Hills is a man-made one: for thousands of years people have lived and worked on and around the hills and their activities have influenced the way the hills are today. From Bronze Age burial monuments around four thousand years old, Iron Age hillforts around two thousand years old to relics of the Cold War from the last century, the historic landscape of the Quantocks is rich and diverse. At the start of this millennium, to better our understanding of both the extent and nature of this historic landscape, English Heritage, Somerset County Council and the

AONB Service set up a project to record the archaeological remains of the hills, culminating in a book by Hazel Riley, *The Historic Landscape of the Quantock Hills.* This details the results of the extensive survey work and places the story of the Quantocks in its regional and national context.

The hills have some impressive surviving prehistoric remnants, still easily seen today: Dowsborough Hillfort, Dead Woman's Ditch, huge burial cairns along the western ridge, Trendle Ring, Triscombe Stone and the ancient, sunken Drove Road, to mention a few. There are medieval manors, such as Kilve and East Quantoxhead on the coast, along with the ancient harbour, limekiln and unusual oil retort at Kilve Pill. In 1924, the Shalime Company was formed to exploit shale oil after a local newspaper reported 'man finds burning rock on beach' here. A retort was constructed in anticipation of this exploitation. However, financial backing for the project failed to materialise, perhaps protecting the beautiful coast here from becoming an early-twentieth-century Dallas!

The post-medieval landscape is one of contrasts. The rolling, pastoral landscape that inspired the Romantic poets Coleridge and Wordsworth was also a working landscape. The oak woods were home to woodsmen and charcoal burners and the fields around Dodington (not far from Wordsworth's home at Alfoxton) were the scene of noisy copper mines in the eighteenth and nineteenth centuries. There were stinking tanneries at Holford, Nether Stowey and Crowcombe, and textile manufacture at Holford and Marsh Mills using water wheels.

The ruins of the old Silk Mills in Holford (along with some moody beach scenes at Kilve) were used in the music video for Bryan Adams' pop-chart success 'Everything I Do, I Do It for You' (the longest unbroken run at number one: sixteen consecutive weeks in 1991). The song was used as the theme music for the Kevin Costner *Robin Hood Prince of Thieves* film. It was interesting to watch this music video being made and I can remember the slightly surreal scene of a grand piano swinging precariously from a crane amongst the old beech trees as it was lowered into the site, and the whole area being swathed in floodlights and atmospheric dry ice 'mist'.

'Wild', Georgian-designed landscapes such as Hestercombe with its temples, lake and waterfall along with its magnificent Edwardian formal gardens (the joint work of design greats Gertrude Jekyll and Sir Edward Lutyens) are also preserved and restored gems, definitely worth a visit, and are beautifully maintained examples of the rich and varied Quantock timescape.

I particularly enjoyed assisting 'the gravediggers' with exploratory digs at Dead Woman's Ditch (prior to erosion repairs), surveying the hills with Hazel Riley and with the University of Winchester when some cropmark enclosures were investigated on the edge of an Iron Age enclosure, surprisingly revealing Roman remains. These turned out to be a Roman villa, complete with a magnificent (and mainly intact) mosaic floor. This is one of the most westerly Roman villas in Britain and the Yarford mosaic dates from the fourth century AD. Saxon graves were also found nearby at Cothelstone, ironically at a place called Stoneage!

Archaeological protection projects include preventing Triscombe Stone from being hit by cars parking at these popular, ancient crossroads. The stone marks this ancient meeting of the ways and probably dates from the Bronze Age; and the word 'tris' is believed to be the Celtic word for 'meeting place'. Travellers and traders have used the Drove Road here since earliest times to trade or move livestock, avoiding the wet, wooded lowlands on either side of the hills. Legend has it that the ghost of a young girl haunts this spot after she froze to death waiting for her beau to turn up on a Lover's Tryst one cold winter's night – he presumably never did.

The area immediately surrounding the standing stone was first carefully surveyed by Exeter University before any works were carried out, and I then had wooden bollards put into the ground to protect the stone. On one of my first days working on the hills I noticed that a Land Rover had driven into this ancient relic and almost knocked it out of the ground! I vowed then to get it protected from further damage.

The only other significant standing stone on the Quantocks is the Long Stone, found at the eastern end of Longstone Hill. It's not very long at all, but has probably been in place for a very long time! It is likely to be a prehistoric (Bronze Age) standing stone, but it also functioned as a medieval boundary stone between the parishes of Kilve and East Quantoxhead.

The stone was recumbent for many years but was re-erected by the Friends of Quantock in the 1960s.

Andy and I were out working at the top end of the hills one day assessing a potential swaling site when we came across a large chunk of smooth, worked stone amongst the charred, black heather stalks of a previous burn. It was half buried on its side in the shallow peat and seemed a little out of place. We extracted it from its resting place and decided it was too good to become lost again (for who knows how many hundreds of years), so we 'rescued' it.

I thought that it would make a great marker stone for a significant trackway junction close by where the northern end of Thorncombe Hill flattens out to meet the head of Bicknoller Combe. We set the stone into the ground in a perfect spot, and it immediately looked as if it had been in *situ* for centuries. Maybe it will be now; a rangers' contribution to a Quantock standing stone. Who knows who were the last people to have set this stone into the ground on that high and lonely place?

I mentioned what we'd done to the archaeologists as I didn't want it to be mistakenly recorded as something much earlier, they were fine about it: just another addition to a long-standing tradition.

It's not only standing stones that were used to mark important routes, boundaries, meeting points or crossroads: timber posts were used too, particularly in areas rich in timber but short on large stones (the Quantocks compared, say, to Dartmoor). Two are marked on the OS map for the Quantocks and are sited high on the open plateau; Halsway Post and Bicknoller Post. Halsway Post had long disappeared by the time I started working on the hills (just a name on a map), and Bicknoller Post was starting to deteriorate. They both marked ancient, important junctions on the old packhorse routes across the open moor. I had them both replaced at the turn of the millennium with locally grown oak, their names carved down their sides. They're very substantial and should last for many, many decades to come. Under each one was placed a coin for future archaeologists to hopefully find and accurately date their installation.

I can remember installing Halsway Post particularly well. The hole had to be deep, about a metre. I was doing my best to retrieve the final clods of earth and stones from the bottom of the hole when my arms buckled and I collapsed into the deep, narrow pit, unable to move. I was stuck, with just my two feet protruding from the hole. After much mirth and an initial pretence of not hearing my muffled cries for assistance, the two heritage team staff helping me with the job literally hoicked me out of the ground vertically by my ankles and held me aloft! Thanks chaps.

Restoration of the significant, buttressed lime kiln in Hawkridge Woods was another success story and is a wonderful example. The stonework was repaired and pointed with traditional lime mortar by experts and for safety reasons a metal grid was placed over the immense drop. An information board and picnic table were installed and a wonderful circular walk through the woods was created from the reservoir below. The bench above the kiln is a wonderfully quiet place to sit with a flask of tea, soak up the woodland environment and gaze across the valley to Wills Neck in the distance. I can almost guarantee you'll not meet another soul. If it's raining, the old, corrugated-iron-roofed kiln burner's hut makes a great shelter. I had always intended to put an owl box in it another job on the 'to do list' for the Quantock rangers or their stalwart volunteers!

Dowsborough Hillfort sits atop one of the highest hills, a commanding position overlooking the eastern flatlands and the patchwork of heath, woods and farmland falling away to the coast. Its ramparts are now clothed in stunted sessile oak woodland and the stunning views from its northern rim can quickly become obscured by scrub. Andy Harris and I decided to clear the main viewpoint so that people could continue to enjoy the views from this lofty and strategic hilltop as they had done for thousands of years.

A Bronze Age burial mound close by (within the ramparts) predates the Iron Age fort. It's interesting to see these two features located so close together, yet two thousand years apart in time.

We needed to take quite a bit of equipment with us, so we used the quad bike and trailer. Once the tree pruning of the viewpoint was done, using a long-handled chainsaw, and after numerous slips into the deep rampart trench, we loaded up the kit and got ready for our descent from the hillfort. I was driving the quad and Andy was in the trailer along with all the equipment. The first section of trackway to negotiate was through deep water so I gave the 650cc Yamaha Grizzly a lot of 'welly'. I didn't see the huge rock submerged in the water and hit it at full speed. The quad leapt into the air followed by the trailer, which bucked and twisted. A brown wave of stinking, muddy water enveloped us. I heard a shout of distress from behind and turned around to see Andy hanging horizontally off the side of the trailer held on only by his trouser belt which had luckily caught onto the frame. Rucksack, camera and most of our kit was in the mucky water and mud!

Phew, how on earth did Andy survive that? He looked a little shaken, but we gathered ourselves and the kit together, had a bit of a nervous laugh, pushed the quad and trailer out of the knee-deep filth and carried on, a little more carefully and a lot muddier! I made for the gap in the ramparts to descend through the oak woods; unbeknown to me the trailer hitch hadn't quite been fitted back on properly. Andy was now sensibly standing at the front of the trailer holding onto the front frame bars; he wasn't falling for that last experience again.

As the ground fell away steeply to our right, I began to steer to the left... unfortunately the quad-less trailer and Andy carried on, dropping steeply to the right. I shall never forget the scene of Andy and the trailer bouncing down the hill through the trees like some phantom, horseless chariot rider. 'Oh no, this is bad.' I stopped the quad and set off on foot, at speed, to try and save him, worried at what I might find.

Thankfully the trailer had come to a stop up against an oak and he looked fine, if not a little shaken. He initially gave me quite a look and then we both fell onto the ground in fits of uncontrollable, hysterical laughter. Andy drove the quad back from there. Let's keep this to ourselves, we thought.

One of my 'special moments' on the Quantocks was finding some worked flints. These were found while I was leading a guided walk in what must be the most remote spot in the hills, near the head of Somerton Combe just below the ageing clump of Scots pine trees known as Stert Firs. As our party climbed up onto the open heath following a narrow sheep path from the ancient woodland in the combe I was plodding along, placing one foot slowly in front of the other. As I looked down, some shiny stone (very different from the local sandstone) in the bare earth caught my eye. Curious, I bent down to pick it up, and discovered that it was in fact two pieces of flint. The nearest naturally occurring flint was at least as far away as east Dorset or Wiltshire… someone must have brought these here.

I wiped them quickly with my fingers and noticed that the edges had been worked into a sharp blade. Was I the first person to handle these in possibly three thousand years?

The find provided a great part of the guided walk, and I was able to talk about the Neolithic hunter-gatherers who regularly visited the hills to hunt deer, boar, bison and auroch. A little south of this spot a hunting camp had been found with worked flints that were used for scraping the skins. Flints may also have been traded for deer antlers by visiting tribes from areas east of the region. I still have those flints safely stored in an old tobacco tin, some of my most precious finds.

Another 'memento' and prized possession I have is an ancient granite anchor or fishing net weight found trapped amongst some rock crevices down on Gorah Rocks near East Prawle back in 1985. This is a beautiful teardrop shape with rounded edges and a chiselled (not drilled) hole. It would have originated in a granite area: Dartmoor, Cornwall, the Isles of Scilly or even Brittany. The South Devon coast has no granite.

Years later, during my first few weeks working for Dartmoor National Park (as part of my induction process) I was allowed to choose another officer to go out with for the day to help me understand what other departments get up to. I picked Lee Bray, the Park's archaeologist. He needed to check up on some recent reports about mountain bike erosion at Grimspound, one of Dartmoor's most important and iconic prehistoric sites. This was before the first Covid lockdown as I remember that we were both in the same car as we headed out into the rolling moors from HQ at Parke. The view opening up over Widecombe church in its beautiful valley setting is always a delight, and I still couldn't quite believe that I was now working in this amazing place.

As a newbie, I enthusiastically and conscientiously quizzed him about his job, which to me seemed one of the best jobs an archaeologist could get. He began by describing how he had got this role and soon described his previous work with Exmoor National Park, so he knew the Quantocks and we soon got into an easy-flow conversation.

It quickly became apparent that we both had pretty socialist views, hated Brexit for all it stood for and were totally unimpressed with Boris and his cabinet of incompetence, chaos and corruption. I felt I'd found a soulmate. Whenever we meet up now, we both end up in 'Victor Meldrew type' rants about the state of everything – we've turned into grumpy old men. It's quite cathartic actually.

Anyway, back to the archaeology... sometime later I dragged Lee out to ask his advice on some major track repairs I was undertaking in an archaeologically sensitive area called Eylesbarrow. The British Mountaineering Council had given us £20,000 through their Mend Our Mountains campaign to help repair eroded paths and fortunately Lee agreed that the work I had in mind was fine. While he was on site, he said he needed to go and have a look at Ditsworthy Warren nearby and asked if I'd like to join him. 'I think you'll find it interesting,' he said. 'We've got everything on Dartmoor, but the gems in our archaeological crown are the prehistoric, medieval and industrial remains. Great stuff.'

We walked out into the open moor, crossing some wet areas and climbed up over a grassy knoll to look down into the yellow grasslands of a rather remote and gentle valley bowl near the head of the River Plym, the brilliant blue line of the sea glinting in the distance. In front of me lay a wonderland of prehistoric remains, a ceremonial landscape dotted with standing stones, some arranged carefully in long rows, others standing like lonely sentinels. As well as stone rows, there were the remains of settlements, hut circles, stone-lined burial chambers and barrows in a bewildering arrangement.

I was blown away. The most impressive standing stones I'd ever seen were just there in the landscape, thousands of years of tangible history right in front of me. We went over to one of the great terminal stones and I couldn't help laying my hands on it and feeling its ancientness, half expecting a deep, distant heartbeat.

The stone is said to be the largest on Dartmoor and stands 4.3 metres tall. Lee explained that these stones could have been originally erected around six thousand years ago by an ancient people speaking a very different language from our own. We walked back along the row of stones up to the top of the valley bowl then sat down on one of the cairns in the warming spring sunshine, gazing south towards the sea, just quietly taking in the ancient amphitheatre below us. I felt privileged to be out with this extremely knowledgeable archaeologist.

I tried to imagine the same view six thousand years ago: willow and alder scrub along the stream banks full of birdsong, smoke curling from turf-roofed round huts, a green swathe of temperate rainforest filling the gap between the high ground and the distant sea, and white-tailed eagles soaring in aeroplane-free skies overhead. It was a truly amazing and unexpected visit; I hadn't expected to see anything quite so mind-blowing only half an hour from where I live, existing relics from a dim and very distant past. Dartmoor and its history are constantly fascinating.

Chapter Eleven: 'Sea and Hill and Wood'

The Quantock Hills are famous (and deservedly becoming more so) for being the birthplace of romantic literature; in particular, the works of the Romantic Poets Coleridge and Wordsworth who lived here prior to them both being accused of spying for the French government and moving up to the Lake District at the end of the eighteenth century. It is in this particular short period of history that they sowed the seeds which inadvertently led to the vision and creation of our protected landscapes today.

Samuel Taylor Coleridge moved to Nether Stowey in 1789 and was soon joined by William and Dorothy Wordsworth who lived nearby at Alfoxton House in Holford. Local film director Julien Temple (of Sex Pistols and Glastonbury Festival fame) made an engaging film about this brief but important period of history, calling it *Pandaemonium*. I was involved with advising on suitable site locations and transporting the actors (including John Hannah, Emily Woofe and Linus Roach) and crew around the hills in my safari Land Rover. It was wonderful to watch this period drama being made and I thoroughly recommend seeing it if you can.

It portrays that, in a way, Coleridge and Wordsworth were the Lennon and McCartney of their day, Coleridge's work perhaps being more creative (undoubtedly being influenced by laudanum) than Wordsworth's. Laudanum was taken at the time as an anaesthetic (Coleridge suffered from toothache and used it as a painkiller), but it was also an addictive opiate and induced hallucinations if too much was taken. The film illustrates how Wordsworth (keen to be made Poet Laureate) recognised Coleridge's skill as a writer and had their major joint work *Lyrical Ballads* published anonymously, not wanting to be overshadowed by Coleridge's remarkable creativity and new style of writing about the landscape and nature.

Coleridge's cottage (opposite The Ancient Mariner pub) in Nether Stowey is now an excellent National Trust Museum and café. It is here in Lime Street that Coleridge wrote some of his best works, including *The Rhyme of The Ancient Mariner, Khubla Khan, Christabel, Lime-Tree Bower* and *Frost at Midnight.* He wrote of the village:

...This populous village!
Sea, and hill, and wood,
With all the numberless goings-on of life,
Inaudible as dreams!

He would regularly walk to visit the Wordsworths close by at Alfoxton, where Dorothy Wordsworth wrote her *Alfoxton Journal* in 1798, combining the intense and detailed observation of nature she witnessed around her with a genuine imagination and poetic flair (presumably referring to Holford Glen):

Wherever we turn we have woods, smooth downs, and valleys with small brooks running down them through meadows hardly intersected with hedgerows but scattered over with trees. The hills that cradle these villages are either covered with fern or bilberries or oakwoods – walks extend for miles over the hilltops, the great beauty of which is their wild simplicity…
…There is everything here, sea, woods wild as fancy ever painted, brooks clear and pebbly as in Cumberland, villages so romantic; and William and I – in a wander by ourselves – found out a sequestered waterfall in a dell formed by steep hills covered with full-grown timber trees.

It gives numerous details of Coleridge's visits, and their visits to him at Nether Stowey, as well as the circumstances under which several of their poems were composed. Many sentences in the journal illustrate an uncanny similarity to words and phrases which occur in William's poems; and there is no doubt that brother and sister must have made use of the same notebook, describing the beauty of nature and the countryside all around them.

Soon after William and Dorothy moved into Alfoxton, Coleridge began to see them almost every day.

The three excited friends wandered the Quantock hills and combes together, discussing their plans to collaborate in changing the course of English poetry. William wrote in *The Prelude*:

Upon smooth Quantock's airy ridge we roved, Unchecked, or loitered mid her sylvan combes.

They would be visited by other 'movers and shakers' of the day, Humphrey Davey and Robert Southey. The Shelleys lived in the rather beautiful Bagborough House, in West Bagborough, which was used in the film as the Wordsworths' home in Holford.

With their unconventional behaviour and their habit of walking everywhere – 'which gentlemen did not do' – it was hardly surprising that they aroused the suspicions of the local people. Who are they? What are they writing in their notebooks? Are they spying for the French?' When John Thelwall, the notorious revolutionary who had been tried for treason, was seen with them in Nether Stowey, there was outrage. The Government sent an agent, James Walsh, down to investigate. He followed them around for a fortnight. Fortunately for them he reported back to London that they were only 'a mischiefuous [sic] gang of disaffected Englishmen', but no real security threat to the country.

The tragic tale of John Walford (the handsome and popular charcoal burner of Over Stowey), whose very human weaknesses led to the loss of his great love, an unwanted marriage, and finally murder and his own execution, acquired literary interest when it came to the attention of Coleridge and Wordsworth in 1797.

The story of John Walford, who was publicly hanged just above Nether Stowey, and his body caged in an iron gibbet (Walford's Gibbet) on the winding, wooded road up to Dead Woman's Ditch, is wonderfully described by the well-known West Country writer Martin Hesp in his book *The Last Broomsquire*. I can thoroughly recommend the read.

The AONB office was moved from the library building in Nether Stowey (originally the old village school, the first purpose-built one in England, provided for by money from Coleridge's friend and neighbour Tom Poole) to the old estate yard at Fyne Court, headquarters of the Somerset Wildlife Trust. The National Trust soon moved their Quantock Wardens and office base here too, so now we had a countryside and wildlife partnership 'team' in one location. Fyne Court was once the home of Andrew Crosse, known as the Thunder and Lightning Man, 'a man humbled by the greatness of nature' and a good friend of Coleridge, Wordsworth and Davey. He wrote:

'It is not merely in the enchanting month of May... or during the rich tints of autumnal scenery, when the purple heath covers the hills with its glorious dyes... it is not merely at that these times that the range of the Quantocks demands admiration... Even the sterile winter possesses adornments'.

It was at Fyne Court that he captured lightning strikes via tall metal poles set up in the trees to carry out his experiments with electricity, the new 'wonder of the age'. He excitedly showed Mary Shelley 'new life' he imagined that he had created, and it is thought that this is where she got the idea for her Frankenstein story.

The main house burnt down in 1894 when a housemaid left a candle unattended that she had been using to heat curling tongs. Servants and neighbours fought the fire before the eventual arrival of the fire brigade, who had struggled with a horse-drawn fire pump all the way uphill from Taunton. The full story of the rather eccentric and intriguing Andrew Crosse unfortunately remains a bit of a mystery, as most of the records and valuable manuscripts outlining the family history were destroyed.

My old boss Ken Brown recently told me that it was he and my father's friend Ernest Neal who rediscovered the old estate yard buildings in the mid-1970s hidden beneath decades of dense laurel and strangling bramble growth. The site had been bequeathed to the National Trust in 1974 by the Adams family and quickly leased to the Wildlife Trust as a nature reserve. After slashing their way through the vegetation and stumbling upon the old, cobbled courtyard Ken and Ernest were astonished to find the old library intact with rows of books still on the mesh-protected bookshelves!

I have had many meetings in that old library room but had no idea of how it came to be rediscovered. The office buildings had a very cheerful Brazilian cleaner called Paulo, and I would often bump into him on my way into work. 'Another beautiful day Tim!' he would cheerfully spout, whatever the weather.

I quizzed him about this one cold, grey winter's day. He told me that he loved the variety of our climate; where he came from it was either very hot or very hot and humid. Every day the weather was now different for him; cloudy, windy, raining, hailing, snowing or bright and sunny, and he adored these differences and seasonal changes. His enthusiasm for the climate that we often moan about or take for granted was refreshing and made me appreciate it with renewed attention.

The Quantocks will always have a special place in my heart. I have particularly fond memories of driving my daughters Rosie and Ellie to school in the Land Rover, for which I obtained special permission from the county council. Their primary school was in the pretty village of Kingston St Mary and there was a choice of route, over the hills, or around the base. The route taken often depended on the weather or how we were doing for time.

The hilltop route took a little longer but was more interesting. We would sometimes pop out of the mist above Tilbury Park into bright blue skies and autumn sunshine and enjoy the stunning views and mainly wooded journey.

'What are those hills over there?' I would ask as we topped the saddle of Birches Corner and much of Somerset would come into view. 'Blackdowns!' they chirped in unison. 'No, try again.' 'Mendips!' 'Yep.' I loved teaching the girls about the environment around them; their childhood felt a little like mine. As we rounded Cothelstone Hill a local buzzard would often drop from its perch and fly along the road just in front of the windscreen, always a welcome sight; it looked so big, like an eagle swooping through the woodland. As we gradually descended towards The Pines crossroads, we seemed to always be singing along to David Gray's 'Babylon' on Radio 2 at the top of our voices.

We would often have to wait as a herd of deer leapt out in front of us from the trees and crossed the road like a fluid brown wave. This was always a good reason for being a few minutes late and reminded me of the excuse my mother used to tell me to say when late for school. 'Just tell them we had to wait for the ducks crossing the road at Whittington Castle again,' she would say. Strangely enough this was occasionally true – and bizarrely I seem to remember them actually using the zebra crossing!

The base-of-the-hills route was safer in snowy or icy conditions or when the hilltops were shrouded in hill fog. It was also fun when flooded, which it often was. The girls loved it when we splashed through the shallow floods, sending a wave over the windscreen or pushing through the longer, deeper ones with a bow wave of water in front of the bumper. Land Rovers really are the best school taxis!

Bringing children up in the countryside is a real privilege (I thank my own parents for making this decision with my brothers and I) and I know that my daughters really appreciate their rural upbringing. A few years ago, I went for a late summer walk with them through the wooded combes and over the purple heath tops near Holford; they said how much they value their childhood growing up in such a wonderful environment. In her autobiography *Search for a Soul,* Phyllis Bottome, in reviewing her childhood, wrote:

The beauty of the waterfalls and streams, the deep red earth, the strong wiry bracken, the low heather hills, the fragrant drenched woods full of moss and ferns: these were the masterpieces of my childhood's world.

After 'leaving the Shire' for university and travel, Rosie and Ellie have both set roots in the West Country, living in Devon and Cornwall respectively, enjoying sea, hill and wood. Like me, I feel that they both have an intrinsic appreciation of nature and the countryside having grown up with it and amongst it as youngsters and being introduced to it by their parents. Long may this generational trait continue.

As a ranger it was imperative that I had an up to date first aid certificate. You never quite knew when you were going to find someone needing attention out on the hills. Twisted ankles, horse riding and mountain bike accidents were common.

Chris and I (along with a couple of colleagues from the Cotswolds) were sent on a paramedic technician course in the Brecon Beacons National Park. One of the course leaders asked if anyone hated needles, and I rather stupidly raised my hand. I was asked to come and sit on a chair facing the other participants and was soon wired up to all sorts of monitors. An extremely long needle and syringe then appeared, and my pulse rate went haywire. This stunt was to illustrate how stress levels affect heart rate apparently.

Fortunately, the needle was not actually used, but I wasn't to know that – in fact I got away rather lightly.

Chris and Jeff suffered a much worse fate: induced hypothermia. They were laid down in a mountain stream for much longer than they should have been. It was early March, and it was freezing. In fact, Jeff had such severe affects from the cold that the course leaders were extremely worried, and he spent the rest of the day recovering. Mouth-to-mouth resuscitation was carried out on casualty 'volunteers' with porridge in their mouths to resemble vomit and our written exam was taken during a snowstorm in a field! A rather intense and testing course, to say the least. We were all extremely relieved when it was over, but we all passed and duly received our certificates.

A rather handy benefit of having this certificate meant that I could volunteer as a first aider with the Festival Medical Services at Glastonbury, a guaranteed free entry to Europe's largest festival. I did this for a few years in the early noughties. The benefits also included a secure camping compound (with electric hook-up), food coupons, our own marquee for eating and partying and, most importantly, flush loos and hot showers! I towed our ancient Abi Marauder caravan there each year; two young daughters loving this annual mid-summer madness. By the time they were teenagers they were hardened 'Glasto Goers' and I'm sure that they will have those long, sunny (or muddy) Solstice days forever soldered into their rather fuzzy memory banks.

I must admit to having taken advantage of my fluorescent medical services tabard and laminated ID card on a couple of occasions while not officially 'on duty'. I managed to gain access to the wings of the Pyramid Stage and enjoyed the rather privileged view of thousands of raucous revellers in front of me as I stood only metres away from Moby and Morrissey during their performances.

Seeing this wonderful crowd highlighted at night by mesmerising laser beams from this iconic, world-famous stage is something I will never forget. It just shows that volunteering your time for something can sometimes reward you. I wasn't overly impressed by Morrissey's numerous and rather pretentious entourage who arrived from LA and posily 'strutted about' backstage, but I remember that his band were brilliant.

Music has always been important to me and has often calmed me in difficult times. The first pop songs I can remember were Nancy Sinatra's 'These Boots are Made for Walking' (being played in a shop in Ellesmere) and Petula Clark's 'Downtown' crackling through the radio of a fin-tailed Ford Anglia. On Saturday mornings we would sometimes listen to Junior Choice with Ed 'Stewpot'. This often featured two little suited pigs on helium, Pinky and Perky, squeakily singing early Beatles covers, dreadful. On occasional visits to Kenilworth to see our cousins, before they moved up to Shropshire, we packed into their local public phone box and called Dial-a-Disc (by dialling 16) and I can remember listening to Elton John's *Crocodile Rock,* just about audible through the receiver.

My first vinyl single purchase was 'Bohemian Rhapsody' by Queen and my first album (I think) was 'Parallel Lines' by Blondie. For my twenty first birthday I treated myself to seeing Simon and Garfunkel at Wembley Stadium, and whenever I hear Paul Simon's 'Late in the Evening' it takes me straight back to the atmosphere of that memorable night in that incredible and now historic venue.

On a hot summer's day with a cold beer in hand, reggae feels right. I also find it helps when you're feeling low; it's a default 'go to' for me when I need to feel basic rhythms in my soul, the pulsing heartbeat of the drums.

I enjoy drums so much that for a while I played Japanese Taiko drums with Kagemusha Taiko at the Phoenix Arts Centre in Exeter. The powerful vibration of these drums is felt in the chest and the reverence that Japanese players give to these drums is spiritual. Not long after playing these I was asked by a colleague if I would play the drums in a local band (as the drummer now played bass). I said I would and soon found myself playing in a band called Antarctica. Playing rock and punk numbers in pubs around Taunton for a couple of years was great fun, and I still miss the energy, joy and camaraderie of playing live music.

I loved my time on the Quantocks – it was a real privilege – but after twenty-five years in that quiet, tucked-away corner of Somerset it was time to move on. On my fortieth birthday, back in 2001, I had been offered the job of Lands Manager with the National Trust on Jersey, a rare opportunity with pink granite farmhouse provided; but after too much um-ing and ah-ing I eventually turned it down. Perhaps we are all allowed at least one regret in our career decisions?

But now I had secured a job with the Woodland Trust as their Site Manager for Avon, Somerset, West Dorset and East Devon, managing some fifty of their sites between Bristol and Exeter; everything from quiet, atmospheric, old woods to well-used community woodlands on busy urban-fringe sites.

My surprise leaving present from my old AONB team (in addition to a wonderful watercolour of Rectory Wood) was a microlight flight. I managed to take this on the last sunny evening of the summer, buzzing out from Dunkeswell airfield on the top of the Blackdowns and shooting out over the sea cliffs near Seaton. Observing scores of metre-wide barrel jellyfish in the blue water hundreds of feet below, following the River Axe back inland and unexpectedly being allowed to steer the nimble flying-machine myself for a while was a joy. However, pretending not to be scared to death as we hedge-hopped at a ridiculously high speed (as a 'treat') towards the end of our flight is something I cannot easily forget!

My new job introduced me to some stunning places: Prescott Pinetum at Uplyme near Lyme Regis with its amazing redwoods; Bishops Knoll, a wonderful hidden garden and woodland (first recorded as a medieval deer park gifted by Henry VIII after the dissolution of the monasteries) above the Avon Gorge in Bristol; and regular drives along the Polden Hills ridge road with its wonderful views of Glastonbury Tor, and the undulating stretch of coast road between Bridport and Abbotsbury (if you haven't driven it, do it!).

Other great drives include the B3306 between St Just and St Ives in Cornwall, the coast road between Dartmouth and Torcross, the truly scenic A39 from Minehead to Lynton and of course, the moorland routes across Dartmoor and Exmoor.

Perhaps not quite so dramatic, but the A361 between Taunton and Street across the Somerset Levels past Burrow Mump can be wonderfully atmospheric with low-lying autumn mists or flooded wetlands, reflecting extensive winter skies.

I was now sharing the old (and rather Gothic) Gamekeeper's Lodge at Hestercombe House near Taunton, reached by a rough track that wound its way through beautiful woods. Being able to wander around Hestercombe estate after the public had gone home and the gates were locked was a wonderful privilege. It was a joy to quietly amble through the rediscovered and restored Georgian landscape area or to sit in the evening sunshine on the Great Plat (a magnificent Edwardian formal garden designed by Lutyens and Jekyll) with a glass of red and a packet of crisps – Lord of the Manor indeed! I have very fond memories of my brief time there.

It is strange to think that when I first started work as Quantock Warden, Hestercombe House was the unlikely headquarters of Somerset's Fire Brigade (probably the grandest HQ in the country). Where the lovely glass-roofed Stables Cafe is now situated was a grubby old stable yard with a set of huge metal ramps for cleaning the fire engines and fleet of old, canvas-topped Land Rovers.

A couple of times each winter I would cautiously drive my own Land Rover up onto these daunting, steeply angled ramps and give it a well-deserved power-wash, 'painting' the surrounding office walls and windows with rust-red Quantock mud!

I now had a new partner Tor, but she lived in South Devon and my twice-weekly commute was beginning to take its toll. Her son Ben was happily ensconced in Modbury's excellent primary school, so for them to up sticks and move home was not a realistic option. Although I had only been in post for about a year, I summoned up the courage to quite innocently ask my boss if I could relocate my home-working office from Somerset to Devon; after all (and somewhat ironically) the South Devon officer lived just down the road in Taunton! The answer was a definite 'No'.

So, after a mutual and rather disappointing parting of ways, I found myself living in Modbury, Britain's first plastic bag-free town. Having started my countryside career in South Devon I had finally returned, and the circle was almost complete – but I needed to get a job. However, limiting myself to a geographical area (that attracted other like-minded job seekers) and not being able to relocate for the foreseeable future, getting one was not going to be easy.

Countryside officer or ranger jobs are notoriously difficult to acquire, and years of funding cuts from government haven't made this any easier. I checked the rare job adverts that occasionally came up but unfortunately most seemed to be time-limited apprenticeship roles, not suitable for me – and certainly not financially rewarding enough to pay the bills!

Feeling a little frustrated (like an out-of-work actor waiting on tables) I exhausted myself working for a landscape gardener and was fortunate to get a three-day-a-week job property managing a large and extremely eerie country house. These jobs tied me over, but I was becoming worried that I would be stuck in this rather unfulfilling rut – and that time was not on my side. I desperately needed a salaried position in my own field of work, and besides, the country house, Alston Hall, was haunted! In its long empty corridors, I would often feel a heavy and persistent presence just behind my left shoulder and the hairs would rise on the back of my neck. I could barely glance up at the black staring windows as I approached the place for fear of actually seeing a face.

I arrived home one drab December's day at half-past four in the afternoon. 'You're home early,' said Tor, rather surprised. 'It's way too scary working out there in the dark,' I said rather meekly. But it was true… it was.

Chapter Twelve: Britain's Ocean City

'Britain's Ocean City': the big road signs depicting Smeaton's Tower lighthouse pronounce as you enter this incredible city, now home to the UK's first National Marine Park, Plymouth Sound. After a year and a half of landscape gardening (mainly in the rain) and looking after the grounds of the very spooky hall (usually on my own) I had a new job at last: Urban Ranger in Plymouth, working for the Devon Wildlife Trust. No more job searching or applications to slave through and a welcome return to a salary, paid annual leave, working in a conscientious and passionate team and, importantly, feeling I was doing something worthwhile with my life again. I barely knew Plymouth. I'd had fish and chips on The Barbican and heard about notorious Union Street; knew that, like my birthplace of Coventry, it had been obliterated during the war, but had no idea just how fascinating and eye-opening this coastal city was going to be.

This was to become one of the most rewarding jobs in my career. It was a partnership role with the Wildlife Trust and Plymouth City Council funded through the National Lottery. The main purpose of the work was to engage residents in some of the most disadvantaged parts of Plymouth with their local green spaces, to increase their health and well-being and to help them improve their environment. In some of these areas the average age at death was ten years below the county average. Unemployment, poor diet, lack of exercise, mistrust of the authorities and detachment from the natural world for generations didn't help. I definitely wasn't going to be preaching to the converted.

As part of the partnership, I was employed by the Wildlife Trust and my partner in crime, Ashley, was employed by the City Council. We were both based at the newly acquired Poole Farm, a remnant of rolling countryside below Derriford hospital. I had to make occasional visits to the Wildlife Trust's headquarters in Exeter and we both had to attend meetings at the City Council's offices near the Mill Bay continental ferry terminal. Although technically employed by the Wildlife Trust, I was working within Plymouth City Council's Natural Infrastructure Team, the NITs.

Poole Farm had been the last of the city council's tenanted farms and was now being developed into an environmental hub. It had some wonderful old outbuildings (including the old milking parlour) and its surrounding land included rare wet woodland and some remnant pastureland with sweeping views towards Saltram Estate and the Plym Estuary.

With soaring buzzards overhead, foxes, badgers and a resident herd of wild fallow deer this was a wonderful working base and excellent example for demonstrating the importance of urban wildlife to visiting groups and schools. Ashley and I very quickly got the three-year Active Neighbourhoods project up and running; positive results, monitoring, statistics and tight deadlines were regularly required by bosses to report back to the partners and funders.

My first day working in the city council offices was a bit of a shock to the system; the Wildlife Trust offices are in a renovated old water mill and the working environment was quite calm. Plymouth's offices, on the other hand, are in a 1980s concrete block, and its open-plan set-up was more akin to a hectic call centre.

As I was being led to my 'hot desk' through the crowded rows of other staff, heads down, punching away at their keyboards, something looked a bit odd. 'I can't see any phones,' I said, initiating some form of observational conversation. 'Oh, we don't use phones, calls are all made through the computer,' said Jemma, my line manager. 'Ah, right,' I confusingly replied.

I was duly given a brand-new headpiece and unwrapped it from its plastic bag. Computer on, login details and passwords sorted out, a few emails out of the way, time to make a call. I eventually found the 'communications bit', searched for the right person in the internal directory, put on my headphones and clicked on to a call to HR regarding the interesting subject of parking space issues.

'HR, how can I help?' 'Err, just ringing to confirm that I have been allocated a parking space for the Active Neighbourhoods ranger vehicle.' 'Can't hear you, can you speak up?' I began to speak at a louder volume (like an Englishman abroad) but wasn't really getting anywhere other than attracting rather annoyed and exasperated glances from the other staff tightly packed in around me.

'Please speak clearly into the mouthpiece,' was the repeated and increasingly impatient response. 'Mouthpiece? What mouthpiece?' 'It's connected to your headphones!'

I took off my headphones to look for the mouthpiece, which turned out to be the bit that I'd put sticking up into the air. I brought it down over my mouth.

'Ah, I'm very sorry,' I said. 'I thought that was the aerial.' More exasperated looks, shaking heads and tutting from all around me. At this point I realised I'd been left behind somewhat in the digital communications world and was rather 'old school'. From that moment on I never used the ridiculous headpiece again, resorting to my Wildlife Trust mobile phone! Apparently, I didn't have an allocated parking space as I had been led to believe.

Part of my new role was to rewrite the management plans for the city's nature reserves. I searched the computer files for the existing ones… wow, they were wordy tomes and a bit dry to be quite honest. They would need a new, concise and more user-friendly approach.

Fairly soon into the new job we interviewed for our first trainee Urban Ranger. This was part of the project's funding requirement of two trainees and a way of training someone into the job and hopefully leaving the legacy of a permanent Urban Ranger for the city. There were plenty of applicants, but Kieran got the job. For the next year and a half, we worked together improving the greenspaces of Plymouth and the health and well-being of many of its residents. We had a second-hand, leased, slightly dented black Toyota Hi-Lux and a black, badged Wildlife Trust fleece each. The Men in Black were now on The Block!

You have to admit that 'Urban Ranger' is a pretty cool job title and we very quickly started to attract attention and become an appreciated addition to the cityscape. Rangers are pretty rare beasts, but urban rangers are an even rarer species, and we were Plymouth's first. We made it our business to get to know our nature reserves and greenspace sites and the sprawling communities that often unknowingly resided adjacent to them. Wonderful places such as Ernesettle Creek, Budshead Wood and Efford Marsh had somehow survived the rapid, mass house-building schemes of post-war Plymouth. Isolated green islands in a concrete Devonian Sea.

Establishing regular volunteer activities and setting up functional Friends Groups was vital to the long-term protection of these areas and the Active Neighbourhoods project success. How to engage possibly disinterested people in these activities was one of the initial hurdles, and then to maintain and ensure their long-term interest in the sites was the next.

Fortunately, Ashley (who had come from a teaching background) was full of ideas! His outdoor cooking activities became legendary. Cooking over a fire bowl, adding foraged blackberries or wild garlic to damper bread or calzone was great fun and we literally had the local residents eating out of our hands! 'You want to get people to come along, give 'em free food!' he said. This formula worked so well that at almost every family or volunteer event we had a fire bowl going, brewed tea and coffee and cooked lovely outdoor food: Plymouth's own mobile alfresco food service!

My old skateboarding skills came to the fore on one occasion down by Sutton Harbour outside the National Marine Aquarium. We were tidying our kit away after doing one of our seashore activities. A rather trendily dressed chap appeared and started to have a chat; he seemed very keen to know what we were doing. His name was Jim, he was in his seventies, had Converse sneakers, a baseball cap and carried a skateboard.

'Nice board,' I said. 'I used to ride one like that once, mind if I give it a try?' 'Here ya go mate', he replied in a London accent, handing me the obviously well-loved board. Despite wearing an old pair of steel toe-capped wellies I did give it a go, much to the disbelief of my colleagues and amusement of some passing members of the public. I jumped on the board, 'tick-tacked' my way up to the aquarium, slalomed back and ended with an almost perfect three-sixty in front of a sign ironically stating, 'No Skateboarding'! I still had it in me, and thank goodness I hadn't fallen off, but I wasn't going to give it a second go just in case. I asked Jim if I could take a photograph of him and his retro board for our Active Neighbourhoods Facebook page, but he said no. He had intended to have a go himself, thought we were council officials and had already been told a number of times not to skate there so didn't want his (rather distinctive) image being promoted. Fair enough.

This incident reminds me of a book I once bought for my younger brother Simon many years ago. It was called *The Answer is Never* by Jocko Weyland, describing the exploits and addiction of anyone who has ever picked up a skateboard. The title comes from the author's own experiences in early 1980s Los Angeles; a rather grumpy old man asks him and his mates, 'When are you punks gonna stop skating on the sidewalk?'... 'Never!' they replied. Hmm... just like me, I thought.

Urban wildlife conservation is without doubt some of the most important conservation work that needs to gain momentum in Britain. More than three quarters of our population lives in towns and cities and many people, possibly a couple of generations, have become detached and dissociated from nature. Engaging or re-engaging people with their local green space is essential if we are to regain an understanding and appreciation of the wildlife often found on our very doorsteps. I know from personal experience that just getting people outdoors can be a life saver.

There have been a couple of times in my own life where I have become very low, effectively depressed (Circumstantial Depression apparently), not able to function, nothing solid to hold onto, unable to even walk. If you can, it helps to acknowledge the fact that the big, wide world still operates without you – night turns into day, winter into spring – in the bigger scheme of things life goes on; many things we think are important are actually quite trivial – do they really matter? Let them go. Getting outside, beneath a blue sky and amongst the living green has saved me. Engaging myself in my local green space, practising what I preach from my own experience – I know it works.

Unfortunately, funding could not be found to extend the Active Neighbourhoods project beyond its three-year programme. This was both disappointing and unsettling. My job as Plymouth's first Urban Ranger came to end in January 2019; but fortunately, within a couple of months I had secured a post with Dartmoor National Park.

Chapter Thirteen: Devon's Granite Heart

On a clear day the northern edges of Dartmoor can be seen from the top of the Quantock Hills, and with binoculars the mast at Princetown (England's highest town) is visible some 60 miles away or so as the crow flies. I often used to gaze at the moor's grey profile on the distant hazy horizon. I had always longed to return to South Devon and working for Dartmoor National Park had always been on my career 'wish list'. Dartmoor is shaped like a heart in the middle of Devon, an amazing granite, tor-topped landscape, with wooded valleys, rushing rivers and picturesque villages that is easy to fall in love with, but takes a lifetime to really know.

With the Active Neighbourhoods project finished I desperately needed employment again, I had a mortgage and bills to pay and my rather ancient and rapidly deteriorating Ford Escort convertible to keep on the road.

I began searching for suitable jobs and signed on to Job Seekers Allowance, receiving a rather eye-popping £73 a week (wow, a tenner a day to keep the wolf pack at bay).

I was beginning to lose faith a little and thinking that I might have to go back to gardening in the rain when I saw a job advert for Assistant Access & Recreation Officer with Dartmoor National Park Authority. It was only four days a week, not great pay and only a year's contract, but perhaps it was my way in. I applied for the post and crossed my fingers; was I overqualified, was there a strong internal candidate, was I too old?

The end of February 2019 was sunny and warm, 21 degrees C, the warmest winter day on record and I went up to London to visit my youngest daughter Ellie who was managing a rather smart, hand-made bike shop in Brick Lane. It was a very 'hipster' area, bearded men with headphones riding skateboards or electric scooters silently side-walk-surfed the streets. We mooched around a bit and breathed in the heavy 'herbal' air. There was a lot going on; it was colourful and cosmopolitan, a very welcome distraction from having no work in conservative, sleepy South Devon.

On returning home a couple of days later I was slumped in bed, rather shattered from the travelling, and saw that I'd missed a call on my phone: it was an old ranger friend of mine on Dartmoor. I decided I'd better just check the message before dropping off to sleep.

'Hi Tim, it's Ian. The National Park wants to know if you're going to be attending your interview at 9am tomorrow morning? They haven't heard back from you.' How had I missed their calls and emails? I panicked a bit.

I rang Ian back; luckily he was working and answered straight away. I explained that I hadn't heard back from the Park and then quickly phoned HR. They were just about to offer my interview slot to the next candidate on the short list. Thanks Ian! Somehow, they had my email address slightly wrong, I hadn't received the invitation for the interview and the Ranger Team Leader had apparently been trying to get me on my phone.

My ancient mobile had been playing up in London and on the train journeys, so I had also missed their calls. They very kindly switched my interview the next day from 9am to 2pm; at least I had some time to prepare. Written test and formal grilling over I drove home an hour later feeling reasonably confident but not really that sure how I had done. Next morning, minutes before leaving for an interview with Plymouth City Council, I was offered the job. I decided to accept it (just as well I did, as I wasn't offered the Plymouth one).

April Fool's Day saw me turning up at the National Park offices for 9am, bright-eyed and bushy-tailed, ready for my induction. The Park HQ is located in a large Georgian house called Parke. This wonderful country pile with its tree-lined drive is owned by the National Trust, leased to the National Park and set within a beautiful, rural riverside estate.

Very different from the city council offices in the heart of Plymouth. I climbed the steps, knocked on the heavy wooden doors set between stone pillars and waited in the warming spring sunshine. I waited and waited; it felt like being an eleven-year-old on my first day in Big School... was I going to be late? I had made an effort to get here in good time, and now it seemed to be going horribly wrong. I would be giving a poor impression by being late on my very first day. I made myself more obvious to anyone looking out of the large windows either side of the doors by standing out on the gravel driveway and shuffling around a little. Eventually I could hear the doors being unbolted; they swung open, and a lady appeared. 'Oh, you're here,' she said. 'Staff usually enter the building round the back.'

I started my four-days-a-week job knowing full well that it only had funding for a year, but had my fingers crossed I could make a good impression and that the role would evolve and increase. Before long I had managed to convince the Authority to increase my four days to five and six months later, I heard that a departmental restructure was looming. A new, permanent post was being created as Recreation and Access Projects Officer, but I would have to apply for it like anyone else. My current post was going to be made redundant – so no pressure then!

I attended the interview. I was pretty stressed – a lot hung on me getting this job. I delivered my carefully prepared PowerPoint presentation, was intensely grilled for an hour by the interview panel and nervously awaited the verdict.

I got the job. I have never felt so relieved to be offered a job. I now didn't have to look for another one and go through those painful, lengthy job searches, applications and nerve-racking interview processes again. A permanent post with a National Park has never been easy to secure and nowadays is particularly rare.

I didn't feel like too much of a stranger at the Park. I had known some of the rangers a long time, mainly through my active involvement with the Association of Countryside Rangers (later to become the Countryside Management Association). They were very much 'part of the furniture' and, once in a job like that why would you want to leave? I can remember seeing one of the rangers (in khaki shorts and shirt) fixing a stile at Two Bridges in the summer of 1985 and jealousy thinking to myself what a great job he had. He's now been with the Park for over forty years!

During a recent site visit with Bill (the ranger for the Haytor area) he recalled some of the wonderful anecdotes of his time on the moor. In his early years as a new ranger, fresh out of college, he was digging in a wooden fingerpost, close to one of the farmsteads. The old farmer came out for a chat, looked at the post carefully, then attempted to give the post a bit of a wobble. 'Firm enough?' quizzed Bill attempting to start up polite conversation, 'I don't know, you tell me, you're the expert,' replied the farmer. 'Could you tie a pig to it?' A fair enough question, I suppose, and obviously a tried-and-tested scale of 'post firmness measurement' passed down the generations out there on the moors.

The same farmer went on to tell Bill how he used to have a bit of fun with the tourists. Like many, he had a public right of way literally running through his farmyard (remnants of historic routes between settlements). Occasionally he would be asked, 'Excuse me, do you know how long it'll take us to walk to Widecombe from here?' 'I'd have to say that all depends on whether you've got a pig or no,' he would reply. 'Oh, definitely without a pig,' they would confirm, slightly taken aback and probably smiling at each other a little. 'Well… I don't rightly know then,' he would ponder for a moment or two. 'I've never actually walked there without a pig before,' leaving the rather bemused tourists to try and work out whether he was being serious or not.

Talking recently with one of the Conservation Works Team, Matthew recalled starting his career with the Park as a young apprentice. He was putting up some signage at Haytor car park, trying to get things straight using a spirit level. 'Hey, what ya doin?' asked his supervisor. 'You don't need to give it a "town job" out 'ere!' I love these stories – they're very 'Dartmoor'.

During some track improvement works, providing wheelchairs and mobility scooters access to the wonderful riverside path at Longtimber Woods (on the edge of Ivybridge), I was having a chat with one of Council's Highways Officers about the difficulties we were all encountering trying to live and work in the new 'Covid World'. 'Hey, you best not go cetchin' thet blimmin' Corvid!' he said.

I did my best to keep a straight face. Hopefully Longtimber's resident pair of ravens hadn't got it! Bird flu maybe.

Providing improved access for people with mobility issues has become a passion for me. As Accessibility Champion for the National Park, I am constantly looking for opportunities to extend this essential provision. In Chapter Ten (The Gravediggers) I talked about my love of history as well as natural history, so working on Dartmoor (which has more prehistoric remains than anywhere else in Europe) has been a real privilege. It is important that everyone should be able to experience this historic landscape; however, some people are not as physically able or mobile as others.

The local Wheelchair Access Group highlighted a problem to me at Merrivale where they had to physically transport their own aluminium bridges to cross the stream so that they could enjoy a circular walk from the nearby car park. A site meeting with the group (in driving, horizontal rain) to look at the problem soon meant that we had a project in the making. This involved finding suitable granite slabs to create two bridges across the stream, allowing access to the stone rows, standing stones and hut circles.

Merrivale is probably the best known and most visited of the archaeological sites on Dartmoor; it is particularly important for its concentration of prehistoric features, so early discussions with the archaeologists and their subsequent approval were vital. Fortunately, they were in full support, along with the landowner. It took a little while, but some suitable granite slabs were found and carefully installed.

Within minutes of being expertly laid they looked like they'd been *in situ* for centuries, fitting into the granite landscape perfectly. To rubber-stamp the work a lone sheep nonchalantly trip-trapped its way across. Job done.

The group were delighted, and the project (Miles Without Stiles) went on to win a national award, featured on local TV (and rather surprisingly, a little later on the BBC national news) with lots of positive publicity on social media. Bridging the barrier from inaccessible to accessible was literally that simple. It doesn't take much to massively enhance people's access and enjoyment of the great outdoors; so vital for everyone's mental health and wellbeing. Who knows when any of us may need small improvements like this to allow us to get out into the countryside and explore?

It is just over seventy years since a forward-looking decision was taken by Parliament to preserve some of our finest landscapes and help people visit and enjoy them. The year 2021 marked the seventieth anniversary of the designation of Dartmoor as one of UK's first National Parks, on 30 October 1951 (the Peak District, Lake District and Snowdonia were also awarded the designation in the same year).

No one invented our National Parks as such; in essence they were already there. But someone had the foresight to recognise their distinction, mark them off as something special, and make sure that the public would have access to them. In a rare book I have, *National Parks for Britain* (commissioned by the Government in 1946) Henry Chessell wrote:

Dartmoor and Exmoor, with the rolling moors rising to characteristic granite tors, fulfil the needs of a national park from the scenic point of view, and the district certainly requires no popularising. Rather it is a question of controlling, however unobtrusively, the use that is already made of it, and preserving it from further vulgarisation...

It seems that Dartmoor and Exmoor were initially considered as one large unit as seen in his list of five potential National Parks for England:

1. *The Lake District*

2. *The Peak District*

3. *The Roman Wall*

4. *The Malvern Hills*

5. *Dartmoor and Exmoor*

His book was written three years before the Hobhouse Report and in 1949 the National Parks and Access to the Countryside Act turned the National Park dream into reality, along with the designation of Areas of Outstanding Natural Beauty (AONBs) and the setting up of our extensive public rights of way network.

After the horrors of two World Wars people needed fresh air, space, and greenery to heal a wounded and traumatised nation. This need is still as vital as ever as we tentatively crawl out of Covid pandemic lockdowns, try to deal with a crippling cost-of-living crisis and assimilate Putin's unforgiveable, illegal and inhumane invasion of Ukraine. Our green spaces (whether urban or rural) and interaction with nature are essential to our mental health and well-being and are arguably as important now as ever before.

A new National Protected Landscapes Partnership has now been proposed by Government, potentially bringing all of our National Parks and AONBs together in one united family, with AONBs being called National Landscapes. As someone who has worked hard to protect AONBs for most of their career I see this as a welcome development. Hopefully, there will be strength in numbers, a new chapter, fairer funding and a positive, successful future for all our protected landscapes.

It's mid-July and I've just been for a cooling, evening swim in a river pool with Tor as the biggest and brightest supermoon of the year (the Buck Moon) slowly rose to bathe the moorland scene below Widgery Cross in a soft, golden glow. Its orange orb reflected a setting summer sun and filled the silent combe, beautifully framed by steep valley sides of heather and rock: a magical and memorable moment.

Dartmoor is a truly unique and special place, much loved by all who come to know it, and certainly worthy of national protection ... well beyond its three score years and ten.

Chapter Fourteen: Legacy

I owe much of my interest in nature to the influence of my father. From my earliest memories of him he was always involved in some committee or other and delivering evening lectures to champion the cause of conservation. He was fighting for the protection of our wildlife when otter hunting, hedgerow removal, badger gassing and gamekeepers' persecution of anything that wasn't 'game' was commonplace and conservationists were often looked upon as 'bearded, sandal-wearing lefties'. He was 'old school' – suit and tie, regularly polished shoes, polite – I don't think I ever heard him swear. His love for the natural world began while on walks with his father, collecting birds' eggs and keeping meticulous nature diaries. He started his career as a conscientious and expert naturalist and became a highly respected conservationist and eloquent educator.

His father, Len Russell, worked in the Triumph factory in Coventry during its car-building heyday. This was Britain's own 'Motor City', producing Hillmans, Jaguars, Daimlers and the beautifully crafted, hand-built Alvis cars.

Len had fought in the First World War. His main role was looking after the horses and he returned home with shellshock (PTSD) from the horrors he witnessed. I can imagine that his nature walks were an essential part of his healing process (if he ever really healed at all). There are some references to him in *Modern Times: World War One*, a history book written by one of my father's late relatives, Steve Gibbons. Steve was able to get real-life recollections of Len's experiences through interviews with him. This was quite an achievement as Len rarely spoke about his traumatic time during the First World War to anyone.

A True Incident

Len Russell raised himself cautiously from his hiding place. The plane had gone, but pandemonium reigned in the camp. Horses were screaming and rearing. Officers shouted orders. He glanced towards the tent. It was in shreds, but the men seemed all right. He turned his attention to the frightened horses. It was a pitiful sight. Some twenty lay on the ground, killed outright by flying bomb splinters. The rest were hysterical. His own horse, Dolly, spotted him as he picked his way across the dead bodies. She lurched towards him, shaking her head vigorously.

'Whoa girl, whoa there!' he said, trying to calm her. She had been struck in the forehead and was bleeding profusely.

Desperately she tried to shake off the protruding splinters. Len patted her on the back and wiped the blood from her face. She screamed and stamped her hoof. Sadly, he made his way with her towards the veterinary surgeon's tent.

There were dozens of horses waiting at the tent, stamping, snorting and whinnying. He tried to close his ears to the sound of the officer's pistol, busy behind the tent. A few moments later the surgeon glanced over the wounds. He shook his head and waved Len and Dolly to the rear. There was nothing that could be done. For Dolly this was the end of the road. For Len this meant parting with the faithful friend of the last two years. The sharp crack of the gun rang in his ears for long afterwards.

One of Len Russell's first experiences of battle also concerned a horse. He was seventeen at the time and had been made 'lead of the gun' – in charge of the horses which pulled one of the howitzers of his battery. It was night-time, and the sergeant's own horse Dixie, was in his care to hold as well as the gun horses. All was quiet. Orders had been given: no smoking, no talking. The signal for action was awaited.

With startling suddenness, a star-shell burst overhead, lighting up all around. In terror, Dixie reared on her hind legs and then bolted. Amid the confusion she was quickly lost in the darkness, and Len never saw her again, though he searched all the following day. He remembered that night more vividly for the sergeant's curses than for the shells which exploded nearby!

Another incident was more humorous. Gas Masks were issued. These consisted of hoods, drawn right over the head and tucked into the neck of the tunic. It was important that the horses grew accustomed to seeing their drivers in these monstrosities: 'We lined up behind the horses. The sergeant barked out the orders, and the masks were hastily donned. We were told to step forward. The horses took one look at us in the masks and shied, reared and bucked in their stalls. It took a long time before they realised who we were.'

Occasionally transport became so bad that fodder and water could not be brought up for days on end, and the animals would be on short rations. But the work of supplying the guns had to go on.

'The order would arrive to take ammunition to the gunners, but the horses were so weak that they could hardly stand. I remember some of them just lying down and "giving their necks". They simply wanted to die. When they did this we had to pour water in their ears to make them stand up'. It was an unwelcome and heartrending task.

Many years afterwards, Len Russell still preserved a vivid recollection of the clinging slime and mud-filled shell-holes of Passchendaele. For my grandfather to have experienced all that horror at such an early age (a teenager) and then to have his home city bombed to oblivion some twenty years or so later while raising a young family is unimaginable. No wonder he drank and smoked! I am glad I can just about remember him – he died when I was nine.

My father's influence on my brothers and cousins during our formative years has led most of us into lifetime careers in nature conservation and an inherent love for the natural world. The more I think about him, the prouder I am of him and the more I mourn his loss. For most of my later teens and through my adulthood I found it difficult to talk about him, 'to go there', to remember and celebrate him; his tragic, untimely death was a massive shock to me, lasting many years and just too painful to revisit. How many birthdays and Christmases have I had without my father being around to share the joys and celebrations? To recognise my achievements, to support me when I was down, to give me wise guidance, to have his grandchildren sit on his knee.

This sadness hit me on Boxing Day about ten years ago. I felt hugely depressed and didn't know how to contain my cumulative grief. I went for a walk down the east side of the River Erme and found myself sitting on the rocky outcrop at the mouth of the estuary and wept uncontrollably, my whole body shaking, a tsunami of emotion pouring out. I slowly let my eyes wander up the river, following its wooded banks through the beautiful Fleet Estate and up towards its lonely, peaceful source up on the moors. I gradually began to feel better, soaking up the timeless scene, comforted by the constant flow of the river, the watery sun slipping into a wintry sky and the cheerful, piping call of the oystercatchers bringing me back into the moment. Nature had rescued me once more, my default sanctuary and saviour.

I have driven the A5 a few times between Betws y Coed and Bangor, through Capel Curig, beneath mighty Tryfan and past the picturesque lake of Llyn Ogwen; this was the country my dad loved as a climber, and it is here I know his spirit soars with the ravens of the mountains. His love of hills and mountains meant that we grew up with them on our doorstep and inherited his love for them; they were always within our horizons and there to explore. We enjoyed countless sunsets from Sweeney Mountain, watching the sun slowly sink behind the Berwyns, leaving an undulating, deep-purple silhouette of landscape. We saw the first dusting of winter snow on the high ground, forming a white rim around the western edges of Shropshire, the lower plain and winding Severn Valley still green below.

Growing up amongst hills gives you an underlying sense for adventure and intrigue. 'What's beyond that ridge?', 'What's the view like from the top of that hill?', 'Let's get up into the snow!' My eldest daughter Rosie and her partner Ben have just returned from a weekend in Snowdonia, climbing up onto Tryfan. Their photos on WhatsApp show them up on the rock-strewn tops in bright, winter-solstice sunshine high above the brilliant white clouds in the valleys below. This was one of my parents' favourite mountains and it fills my heart with joy that my father's love of these hills has passed down through two generations already, keeping his memory and influence alive.

A wonderful living legacy he leaves for future generations is Sweeney Fen, one of the most exquisite flower meadows in Shropshire. He discovered its ecological importance when we lived on Sweeney Mountain; it is the southernmost site for the alpine plant globeflower (an Ice Age survivor), its spherical flowers a soft, glowing yellow. In May, the star-shaped flowers of bogbean appear, fringed petals opening white from dark pink buds. Thousands of fragrant orchids flower in early July; tall spikes of purple-pink, along with hundreds of dusky-petalled marsh helleborines, marsh orchids and wild angelica.

A recent BBC *Countryfile* programme showed hay, cut and collected from the fen, being spread on several adjacent fields in the hope that the seeds of some of its extraordinary plants will grow and flourish beyond the nature reserve, extending its beauty and its value for wildlife; literally 'spreading the seeds of conservation', just like my father had done through his educational work and influence. That feels right somehow.

Becoming a father myself was a magical, life-changing moment. I remember 'walking on air' out of Musgrove Hospital in Taunton into the dazzling brightness of a glorious autumn morning. I felt the warmth and golden glow of the rising sun on my face and for the first time felt the comforting presence of my father at my side. I'll never forget it.

Writing this book has been hugely cathartic for me, a significant healing of this deep wound and an important recognition of why for many decades I have been unable to fully 'let go', to drop my protective shield, to be at peace with myself and allow myself to get close to important people in my life.

My brothers and I recently planted an oak tree in my father's memory at the end of my mother's garden in Ellesmere, helping to put some closure on his death at last; as we boys didn't attend his funeral back in 1975. The planting of an oak is a very fitting and long-lived living memorial to him. He never got to write his New Naturalist Series book on *The Otter*, but I feel that at least I have managed to put something down on paper now, recording some of my conservation career, its ups and downs, and bringing his legacy back to life.

After graduating from Exeter University my youngest daughter Ellie worked a season as Beach Warden at Slapton, teaching environmental education from a pop-up trailer on the beach, and Kieran (my apprentice at Plymouth) has just started a new job as ranger for the Nature Reserve, the next generation helping to protect this wonderful place. The place I first started my countryside career, and very special to me.

As I write this section, on the first World Rewilding Day, I feel that there is hope for our nature and countryside and that the practice of ecosystem recovery on a landscape scale and 'wilding' our towns and cities is the way forward. It is also something that has captured the public's emotion and imagination, and that is vital. If the devastating Covid-19 experience has taught us anything, it is about better understanding our increasingly fragile relationship with the natural world and our own mortality. Our arrogant belief that we are the 'super species' who can bludgeon its way forward and selfishly strip the natural resources of a finite planet is clearly absurd.

Fortunately, the tide is beginning to turn. Many people now realise how vitally important it is to value and protect nature as well as being able to enjoy it, particularly as mental health and well-being have been so undeniably challenged during the pandemic, climate and cost of living crises, recession and other global uncertainties. It is important to try and keep ourselves healthy and not take our own lives for granted; 'seizing the day' seems more relevant now than ever.

Everyone, everywhere, should be able to grow up, and grow old with nature and have the opportunities to experience the joy of it in their daily lives. My mother recently sold her much-loved and well-used campervan. A sticker on the back read 'Adventure before Dementia'… I'm going to adopt that advice over the next few years, just in case!

I would like to think that during my own career I will have left a positive mark on the places and people that I have come into contact with and care about. Having just visited the Quantocks after being away for a few years, it was a heart-warming experience to walk the deep combes and broad ridges once again on a sunny spring day, the hills simply stunning in their natural beauty.

Driving around the lanes I could see that the old cast iron road signs I had restored some twenty years ago were freshly painted, the village gateway signs I had designed and installed were still in good condition, and young saplings that Chris and I had planted thirty years before were now significant trees. A sunset stroll up onto Cothelstone Hill revealed that the Exmoor Ponies had four new foals to help keep the herd healthy into the future. The hills were in good hands.

It's mid-September 2022, the weather's glorious, and Tor and I are in Oxford for a few days break. The golden glow of early autumn sunshine on honey-coloured stone, cycling students, cobbled side-streets and friendly bustle of the old covered market bring back happy memories of my undergraduate days here forty years before.

Much has happened since then; the Queen has just passed away after seventy years on the throne, marking the end of an era. Even monarchs are mortal, and a new chapter for Britain is about to unfurl. The solid continuity of Oxford's ancient walls and its annual influx of new students reminds me that we are only brief inhabitants on this incredible planet and that we can make a positive difference in looking after it as its custodians if we chose to.

A Red Kite soars in low, lazy circles directly above the city garden as I sip my morning cup of tea, what better symbol of renewal and hope (since their re-introduction nearby more than thirty years ago)?

I feel lucky to have had the opportunity to carry the baton that was so tragically taken from my father. Hopefully I have instilled that same sense of wonder for nature and love of the countryside in new audiences and the next generation, who will have a better understanding and appreciation of the natural world and their responsibilities in protecting it.

For ever, for everyone.

Colin Lawrence Russell 1934 – 1975

Moving into Preston Montford Hall (1973) along with dog, goat, and chickens

Lawrence Henry (Len) Russell 1897 – 1970

PART OF THE FUNDS USED IN THE
FURNISHING OF THIS BARN WERE DONATED
BY FRIENDS AND RELATIONS IN MEMORY OF
COLIN RUSSELL
HON. SECRETARY SHROPSHIRE CONSERVATION TRUST
1966 – 1970 · CHAIRMAN OF ITS EXCUTIVE COMMITTEE
UNTIL HIS DEATH IN A ROAD ACCIDENT IN 1975

THE EDUCATION OF CHILDREN AND ADULTS TO A
BETTER UNDERSTANDING OF THE COUNTRYSIDE
WAS VERY DEAR TO HIS HEART.

**Plaque rescued by my brother Simon from Earl's Hill Barn
during change of use.**

15: Suggested Walks

I have compiled six walks, two from each of the areas that have been special to me. I would recommend taking an OS Explorer map with you and some binoculars (just in case).

South Devon AONB - OS Explorer OL20

Start Point and Mattiscombe Sands:

If there was ever a walk to really clear the head and raise the mood, this has to be it, my default walk when a good one is needed! This 3 km circular walk from Start Point car park (GR 820375) includes views of the iconic ridgetop lighthouse, sweeping seascapes, rugged coastal scenery (often with seals and sky-diving gannets) and a beautiful beach. Clear weather views sometimes allow Portland Bill in Dorset and the Lizard peninsula in Cornwall to be seen.

Route description:

1. Exit the car park through the gate next to the information board and follow the tarmac road down towards the lighthouse.
2. Just after the wooden shed (on right) follow the South West Coast Path finger post direction to Minehead!
3. Follow this small path all the way around the cliffs and headland to Mattiscombe Sands. Just before reaching the beach keep a lookout for seals on the rocks just off the headland.

4. The path back up to the car park follows the valley above the beach.

Distance 2.5 miles. Pay on entry car park. Public toilet in car park (summer only).

Toby's Point, Ringmore:

One of Tor and mine's favourite local walks. Wonderful views of Burgh Island to the east and the near-vertical, shiny Devonian Age rocks in the cliffs above Ayrmer Cove to the west. This is a very easy, linear 1.5 km (there and back) route in its own right but can be extended by dropping down onto the beach at Ayrmer Cove and walking back up the gradually rising path (on the east side of the valley) or cross the stream over the wooden bridge and walk back via the village and the Journey's End pub (2.5 km in total). Useful information board at the far end of the car park. Start and finish at the National Trust car park, in Ringmore (GR 650 457).

Route description:

1. Exit the car park next to the entrance, following the finger post to Coast Path. Turn right and follow the second trackway on your right.
2. Follow this level path all the way to Toby's Point (viewpoint and bench, half a mile). Towards the end of the path look along the top of the dry-stone wall as there are sometimes adders basking here on sunny mornings.

3. To return, just retrace your steps or drop down to Ayrmer Cove beach and follow the path back up to the car park.

Quantock Hills AONB - OS Explorer 140

<u>Heart of the Hills</u>:

This 8 km circular walk is an old favourite and I used to include this in our seasonal guided walks programme. It takes in some of the best of Quantock, rushing streams, wooded combes, open heaths, expansive coastal views (often to the Brecon Beacons) and a picturesque village. A good chance of spotting wild red deer. A walk that would have been very familiar to Coleridge and the Wordsworths in their wanderings and has probably changed little since. The walk starts and finishes in the village of Holford (just off the A39).

Route description:

1. From the Bowling Green car park (GR 154 411) turn right back onto the lane, over the bridge and follow the path to the right of the row of thatched cottages. Turn right again and follow the lane all the way until the tarmac ends next to Holford Combe Hotel. (Look out for the old mill water wheel).
2. Carry on through the wooden gate/gap and follow the track up into Holford Combe. Follow the path-side stream until a large clearing is reached (GR 155 391). This is a wonderful glade (a likely stag rutting ground),

a meeting of the ways and a good place to stop to catch one's breath and maybe grab a drink.

3. From here, almost turn back on yourself and follow the path that forks off gradually uphill to the left in a NW direction (**not** the path heading off up Frog Combe). Follow this uphill path through the woods until you break cover. Keep following the same path until it reaches a much wider path on Hare Knap.

4. Turn left up to the crest of the hill and bear right to the cairned summit of Higher Hare Knap. Now this really is a great spot to take a well-deserved break, get out some snacks and pour out a coffee from the Thermos!

5. From the cairn take the grassy path in a NW direction towards Lower Hare Knap. At a path 'crossroads' (GR 147 399) turn left and drop down into the woods of Somerton Combe. Turn right once the valley floor is reached and head downstream.

6. At the next junction of paths head west under Lady's Edge up Sheppard's Combe. Follow this quiet valley all the way up to the very top at Bicknoller Post (GR 128 403).

7. From Bicknoller Post (replaced to commemorate the Millennium) head east out along Longstone Hill. Follow this ridge all the way to the grassy look-out (just before the pine tree memorial) at the top of Willoughby Cleave.

8. Drop down the steep stony path through the trees until you reach the wide stream at the bottom of the valley.

9. Ford the stream and follow it all the way back beside the track down Hodder's Combe into Holford and the Bowling green car park.

Lydeard Hill and Wills Neck:

A wonderful 4.5 km 'figure of 8' hilltop walk in the southern half of the hills, taking in Wills Neck and Lydeard Hill the two highest hills being (386m and 364m respectively). Extensive views are afforded across much of Somerset to the Mendips, the Blackdowns, the Brendons and even to distant Dartmoor on the southern horizon. The walk begins and ends in Lydeard Hill car park (GR 181 331) above the pretty, red sandstone village of West Bagborough (and great pub, The Rising Sun).

Route description:

1. Leave the car park by the main gate and immediately bear right following the path up onto Lydeard Hill itself (**not** the main track alongside the fence on the left, this is utilised on the way back).
2. Once on the ridge bear left and follow the hilltop to the gate in NW corner (back onto the main track). Go through the gate, pass the path immediately on your left (that drops into West Bagborough) and take the gateway into the woods on your left.
3. Follow this path, keeping the old beech trees to your right, gradually head NE to exit the woods in the top corner.

4. Climb out onto the open heath and join the main track that heads along the wide ridge to the trig point and summit of Wills Neck (GR 164 352). Enjoy the view. It is worth walking a few metres beyond the trig point to get a view along the western scarp towards Minehead and the coast.
5. Backtrack about 200m from the trig point and take the path on your left that drops down towards Black Knap. On reaching the old trackway (100m) at the bottom turn right and follow this main track all the way back to the car park and the beginning of the walk.

Dartmoor National Park - OS Explorer OL28

<u>Dartmeet river walk:</u>

This 2km (there and back) walk down the east side of the Dart has been a family favourite for many years and quite sheltered on a blustery day. It starts and finishes at Dartmeet car park, refreshments and toilets (GR 672 732). It takes in the beauty of the River Dart where the West and East Dart sections meet and follows this lovely stretch of river (through Devon Wildlife Trust's Dart Valley Nature Reserve) to a series of waterfalls and rock platforms set amongst ancient oak woods below Combestone Tor. If you follow the path for just over 1km you will find the spot where the path comes down to the rocky edge of the river. Here you will find the waterfalls and rock platforms that extend into the river - the perfect place for a picnic!

Please Note: *The path is clearly defined for most of this walk but uneven and rugged so wear comfortable walking boots if you have them. The riverside boulders can be very slippery.*

Route description:

1. Leave the car park via the main entrance, carefully cross the road and take the path down the left hand side of the river. It bends around to the left, follow this and go through the gate.
2. Follow this path all the way along the riverside, passing Combestone Island until you enter some birch and oak woods, and the ground flattens out.
3. Stick to the main trail through the trees and gradually bear right down towards the river below (GR 675 722).
4. Once down at the water's edge you will find a series of small waterfalls and rock platforms.
5. Return via the same route.

Haytor Quarry & Smallacombe Rocks

The short walk up to Haytor Quarry (1 km there and back) from the Middle carpark (GR 764 772) is definitely worthwhile, it's a magical place and very sheltered in prevailing winds, so ideal for a picnic. A walk out beyond the quarry leads to Smallacombe Rocks, a further 2 km there and back (GR 756 783) allowing wonderful views of Hound Tor, surrounding moorland and the Becka Brook valley.

Route description:

1. Follow the track across the road from the car park all the way up to the gate into the quarry (this is a great spot to turn around and appreciate the views to the south and east all the way to the coast and the South Hams).
2. Go through the gate and into the quarry.
3. Keep to path and exit via the gate on the northern side.
4. Follow the grassy path until you meet the old granite tramway and head out towards Smallacombe Rocks (again a great place for a coffee break or picnic).
5. Return via the same route or take a detour around the back of Haytor itself.

Plymouth 2018

Hope you enjoyed the read - Tim